SINGULAR VESSEL
OF DEVOTION

SINGULAR VESSEL OF DEVOTION

THE SACRAMENTAL BODY AT PRAYER

Paul Janowiak, SJ

Paulist Press
New York / Mahwah, NJ

Library of Congress Cataloging-in-Publication Data
Names: Janowiak, Paul, 1951– author.
Title: Singular vessel of devotion : the sacramental body at prayer / Paul Janowiak, SJ.
Description: New York ; Mahwah, NJ : Paulist Press, [2021] | Includes bibliographical references and index. | Summary: "An exploration of the incarnate mystery of the sacramental Body of Christ gathered for prayer"— Provided by publisher.
Identifiers: LCCN 2020037169 (print) | LCCN 2020037170 (ebook) | ISBN 9780809155095 (paperback) | ISBN 9781587689086 (ebook)
Subjects: LCSH: Jesus Christ—Mystical body. | Worship.
Classification: LCC BV600.5 .J36 2021 (print) | LCC BV600.5 (ebook) | DDC 262/.77—dc23
LC record available at https://lccn.loc.gov/2020037169
LC ebook record available at https://lccn.loc.gov/2020037170

ISBN 978-0-8091-5509-5 (paperback)
ISBN 978-1-58768-908-6 (e-book)

Published by Paulist Press
997 Macarthur Boulevard
Mahwah, New Jersey 07430
www.paulistpress.com

Printed and bound in the
United States of America

CONTENTS

FOREWORD

We have tested and tasted too much, lover–
Through a chink too wide there comes in no
wonder.

Patrick Kavanagh, "Advent"

EVERY NOW AND AGAIN, you find a book that addresses a myriad of issues through the lens of one central insight. And as you read, conversations, formation challenges, theological conundrums, and even personal struggles surface, and, at least in part, are laid to rest, as that one key truth weaves its way, from start to finish. Paul Janowiak's *Singular Vessel of Devotion* is such a book, and one that the fields of liturgical studies and theological formation have long needed. It is theologically grounded, rich, slow-cooked food about realities that are both every day (*cotidiano*) and yet at times really hard for us to "taste and see": the God in whom "we live and move and have our being" (Acts 17:28) has chosen to become present in our local, concrete, eucharistic communities, when we are drawn into the reality of Jesus's surrender to his Father, in the embrace of the Spirit.

Devotion is not a fashionable word in most theological circles. It can evoke individual pieties too often set against "intelligent," historically informed understandings of Christian spiritual practices. Yet undeterred, Janowiak sets us on a pathway to comprehending the theological heart of how praying shapes believing and informs a life (*lex orandi, lex vivendi*)—this time the life of the sacramental body at worship, a soul-in-communion. In this key, *devotion* plays out as that "singular and profound dedication to the Other and to the Body's participation in that communion that flows from the Trinity's own way of being" (p. 22).

vii

Christ's own mind, love, and kenotic self-giving set the tone of, or rather, choreograph and carry the interior attitude of a worshiping community within and into God's loving presence. The focus here is on the reality of our shared belonging to Christ, and how perhaps the most scandalous of all real presences of Christ—and the most challenging for our postmodern, individually shaped freedoms—is the one that fills the building when a worshiping community gathers in prayer. Our communal prayer and devotion is "spiritual choreography" in which "the individual steps back and a new Body begins to move as one" (p. 52).

Why is this important? And who will benefit from this book? From the standpoint of my work on theological aesthetics, on the one hand, and theological formation of future ministers, on the other, I suggest the book has important contributions for two areas or audiences. For the academy, it invites and challenges us to reintegrate the prayerful, the aesthetic, and the exploratory with conceptual understandings of human knowing and believing. Janowiak's theopoetic style of writing, combined with his grasp of the embodied nature of human understanding, spiritual praxis, and theological insight, is refreshing, to say the least. But it also opens doors to rethink central aspects of our faith in ways that are essential for the effective transmission of faith *and* doctrine to the future generations. We cannot continue to pretend that the ever-diminishing world of theoretical thought patterns suffices for theology to adequately perform its function!

The second audience who will benefit from the book are those at the coalface of ministry, the current and future ministers whose role it is to lead our eucharistic communities, as well as those whose role it is to help "form" or train them for that ministry. Differences of opinion, not to speak of battle lines drawn, are evident around the world, from the Vatican to most local churches. I believe Janowiak's book presents a framework that can help us to overcome current unhealthy (and untruthful) polarizations in liturgical preferences and positions. He goes behind the rubrics—not to remove them but to situate them within their theological and spiritual context in a way that enables the conversation about *how* to faithfully interpret and celebrate the mysteries of our faith. For those in formation for future ministry (and those of us who work *with* them), it offers clear points of reflection that enable us to *not* sacrifice prayerful celebrative modes to lowest-common-denominator inclusion, or vice versa, genuine appreciation of the community as primary celebrant to the authoritarian whims of each main celebrant.

Foreword

I have often thought that the doctrine and *reality* of the Body of Christ and the whole Christ (*totus Christus*) is underestimated and under-explored in contemporary theology and spirituality. In this book, it is the air that we breathe. In fact, it is this spiritual core that animates every practical and actualized suggestion on words, space, or liturgical gesture. We are the Body born of the side of Christ, vine and branches, Head and members, *the* place par excellence of God's encounter with God's people. Jesus is not far from us, hidden in some spiritual form invisible to earthly eyes. "Easter visitation and life is not a game of 'hide and seek' the resurrected Lord is playing with the community of believers, but a presence *to* them and *with* them and *in* them" (p. 5). Rather, the resurrected Body of Jesus is to be found, alive and well, visible and breathing life into a world that needs it, through the human, contingent, vulnerable, diverse but one reality of every Eucharist community, even as we reach toward being who we are!

This foundational reality is the *cantus firmus* of this book. For that reason, *Singular Vessel of Devotion* is a book we shall need to read in the same spirit it was written, a spirit of faith. Theology is usually more explanatory than exploratory. In the many spaces we call post-Christian, theologians find ourselves explaining our thought, bridging the language of faith, philosophy, and doctrine as best we can to the world in which we live, unequipped for the inherited terms we work with. This kind of translation of theological language and insight is an essential task, but it is not the only way of theologizing. Janowiak's book, in his own words, offers us a meditative theology, and needs to be read similarly, in contemplative mode. As such, it is a book to taste as much as to comprehend, but that does not make it unpractical! Janowiak reflects upon and addresses key issues of liturgical celebration—such as the role of the presider, the organization (and orientation) of the people of God in the worship space, and the place of the altar, baptismal font, and ambo—in tones that do not ring forth as if from an ideological pulpit of preconceived ideas or received habits, or even solely from contextualized personal or communal experience, but from a prayerful, theologically informed and felt understanding of the people of God in a unifying, sacramental way of praying, acting, and being.

Janowiak explores the sacramentality of word, gesture, and place as an embodied, participative, and relational space we create and which, in turn, re-creates us, because "matter matters and form forms"! This is one of the key principles guiding attentive discernment of the external elements of our liturgical spaces: what we do, how we move, where we stand, when we speak or remain silent (to listen), our choice of adornment or lack thereof; *everything* we do is important because here, the inner and outer dimensions of life are in a mutually transforming relationship, a circular dynamic in which the hidden life of Christ's body graces each expression, at the same times as its bonds are *intensified* in and through that same act. Even the place within which we gather becomes sacred *through the practice of the sacramental body.*

This attentive awareness grounds an eloquent contribution to our understanding of the role of the presider—that most debated role!—as one who *never* speaks in his own name but gathers the assembly through the voice of Another. For some years now, work on a renewed theology of priesthood has been crying out for attention, and this book offers an important contribution to the theme. Voices can reveal or mask the truth. *Only* faith-filled and self-emptying surrender to the Other at the center of the whole Christ in worship enables a community to recognize and resonate with the voice of the Good Shepherd in the timbre of the presider's gathering call; "they will *not* follow a stranger" (John 10:5, emphasis added). Similarly, the gathered community is challenged to reimagine its own role in the worshiping space: solitary Christians who claim their baptism while shunning commitment to a concrete sacramental community thwart the life and growth of the Body of Christ in this world. And the challenge is not only an inward-looking one but affects the mission of the Church in the world! Even as the book opens one's imagination to rediscover the height and depth of the meaning of our liturgical life, the reality of our actual practice is mirrored, and the consequences of its deficiencies uncovered. How can the world access the embodied sacramental presence of Christ through the assembly, if we are not, in our diversity, an embodied soul-in-communion?

This is an important book, and a prophetic one. In fact, it may become a classic for those for whom prayer is the only access point to the meaning of life in Christ, and the celebration of the Eucharist remains our personal source and summit, even as we struggle with how it is sometimes celebrated. Paul Janowiak's prayerful "attentive intentionality"— and I am blessed with the memory of numerous shared celebrations with him that have colored and given flesh to my own reading of this exceptional book—invites us to reimagine our life in Christ. It allows us, in the words of that most sacramental of all Irish poets, Patrick Kavanagh, to reenter the hidden room where love abides, and taste afresh the wonder of how loved we are!

Dr. Maeve Louise Heaney, VDMF,
Director, Xavier Centre for Theological Formation,
Australian Catholic University
August 29, 2020

PREFACE

You should know how to behave in the household of
God, which is the church of the living God....Undeniably
great is the mystery of devotion,

> Who was manifested in the flesh,
> vindicated in the spirit,
> seen by angels,
> proclaimed to the Gentiles,
> believed in throughout the world,
> taken up in glory. (1 Tim 3:15b-16; NABRE)

THIS BOOK EXPLORES the incarnate mystery of the sacramental Body of Christ gathered for prayer. Its approach is a meditative theology that begins from the inside out and employs the richness of the liturgical tradition and practice as an expression of that interior dynamism. A meditative theology of liturgical praying takes seriously and reverences the spiritual fruits that take root and blossom when a faithful gathering for prayer is at the core of the Body's life and rhythm. The sacramental Body is shaped from the inside out by the Spirit's hallowing and Christ's intimate, "real presence," the Son's obedient response in praise and thanks to the Father's love. She gives embodied witness to this dynamic enactment, which announces, first and foremost, a divine initiative and encounter. Liturgical praying, therefore, is a graced trinitarian encounter, whose "mystical unfolding"[1] is rooted in the pierced heart[2] of the Father's loving desire to be with his Beloved, who "was manifested in the flesh," the incarnate Word of God, who now summons and blesses those who gather through the impelling movement of the Holy Spirit. The sacramental Body at prayer, therefore, is a symbolic expression of this communion,

xiii

truly *a singular vessel of devotion*, to use an image of the Church that will unfold throughout this book.

In the beginning of the Gospel of John, we hear the words of Christ, who is at the center of this sacramental Body, asking the primordial religious question to the two disciples in a way that can be a fresh hearing for us: "What are you looking for?" he asks them, and then Jesus invites them to accompany him, to "come and see" (John 1:38–39). In response, Andrew and his companion follow him and a community is born, rooted in Christ. Notice the nascent ritual pattern and its dynamism: call and response, looking intently and seeking in active engagement, and a communal joining in the journey, a response to a summons whose future is full of hope, but whose direction is not all that clear. In short, it is a call to a living faith. The sacramental Body of Christ to this day is the fruit of this communion, the Trinity's own way of being for us, never isolated from us in its loving identity.

In every age, this communion takes flesh in the Head and members, gathered in his name, through and with and for one another. He is in us and we are in him. The sacramental Body of Christ, in union with her Lord—the "whole Christ" (*totus Christus*)—is the primary celebrant and communicant in any liturgy. She is praying, not just says prayers or follows common rubrics. The "mystery of devotion" of which Paul speaks in 1 Timothy begins inside and finds its way and truth and life in community, communion, and mutual sharing of the gift of self, the *whole* self, body and soul and mind and heart. This profound union takes preeminent sacramental shape in the gathered Body of Christ and is renewed "from age to age," which nourishes the mystic bond through each enactment. "Praying shapes believing and informs a life" (*lex orandi, lex credendi, lex vivendi*), and the circle of this mutual unfolding of grace deepens. Let us return again to that primordial meeting in John.

> And the Word became flesh and lived among us, and we have seen his glory, the glory as of a father's only son, full of grace and truth. John testified to him.... (John 1:14–15a)

The Lamb of God's invitation to the disciples in John evokes a response. They look at him and find in him a heart-to-heart resonance, and so "they followed Jesus" (1:37), initially stirred by the redemptive preaching of John the Baptist. They are moved to ask him about the place where he lives: "Where are you staying?" (1:38). Such a question signals the advent of a process of initiation into a new life with a glorified vision. It is asked today with the same fervor, whenever the Church gathers in his name. Truly, we might ask ourselves, where *does* the Redeemer abide? Where does the Promised One dwell among us? This book focuses on that search, and the privileged setting is the praying assembly who meets him in the proclamation and hearing of the word, and in the breaking and sharing of the bread and covenantal cup, where word and table are the testifying locus of our holy communion in him.

The liturgical tradition names this encounter in every space and time as "a perfect offering of praise and thanks"; such praying is "truly right and just," and it is *perfect, fitting,* and *right,* not because we do these deeds in a rubrical, precise fashion, but—first and foremost—because we are in consort with Christ, who is acting as the Head of this Body, offering himself and animating the whole Body as a perfect eucharistic gift to the Father. Beyond what our senses can comprehend (*sensuum defectui*), as Aquinas sings,[3] Christ the Head is also the heart of this true and mystical Body, the animating center and wellspring. This is wholeness at worship, inside and outside, a sacramental bond within a sacramental Body.

The depth and intimacy of the mystery here should not be passed over lightly. A fragile and broken people, swept up in a passionate and yet tender act of redemption, and now gathered to her Lord in intimate union, is the dynamic locus of this mystical unfolding of grace. Here the scandal of the incarnation is most explicit, where the heart and head and soul of Christ sanctifies and animates the whole Body. And so we dare to proclaim that the redeeming Lord is really and truly present, close to us in our praying and worshiping, because this is God's redemptive way of communicating saving life to us. Through the Father's own fashioning, Christ, proclaimed in the creed as "God from God, Light from Light,"[4] illumines the Father's own loving desire for us by sharing our humanness. The Lord of all creation chooses to draw near to be the companion who knows our weakness and shares our sorrows, who hands over his life, all so that as the Body of Christ we might enter the holy of holies *per ipsum, et cum ipso, et in ipso* ("through him, with him, and in him"). The Body, in this self-offering, has a synergy with her Redeemer. Like the disciples, we "follow him" in this sacramental action, "hold fast to our confession," as the Scripture exhorts us, and we humbly "approach the throne of grace with boldness, so that we may receive mercy and find grace to help in time of need" (Heb 4:14, 16). Because of this mutual indwelling, it is right and fitting and just to render praise and thanks, to invoke the Father almighty in one doxological voice, and announce that "in the unity of the Holy Spirit, all glory and honor is yours, for ever and ever!"

THE COMMUNAL IDENTITY DEEPENS IN THE DOING

Starting from the inside dynamism and moving to its outward expression, we reverence and give intentionality to the fashioning of the Body. "Where do you stay?" we echo with the first disciples, as they set out to follow him. We "hold fast" to our companion, and Christ—in a merciful, self-emptying love—clings also to us, his spirit-filled resurrected Body in the world. The liturgical gathering announces this incarnate reality and such praying sustains and nourishes the Body; its ever-flowing grace is our lifeblood and our sinew. Eucharist is who we are and what we do in Christ.

> The cup of blessing that we bless, is it not a sharing in the blood of Christ? The bread that we break, is it not a sharing in the body of Christ? Because there is one bread, we who are many are one body, for we all partake of the one bread. (1 Cor 10:16-17)

The eucharistic rhythm and pattern of the liturgy bodies forth Christ's invitation to a relational presence within the beloved assembly. The gathering rites already carry within them the intensification of the covenantal bond of sacramental presence, bidding the triune God to be with us through the hallowing of the Holy Spirit, allowing us to be willing receptors of the overflowing love between the Father and the Son, which is now our own baptismal inheritance and identity. "In the name of the Father, and of the Son, and of the Holy Spirit" is the beginning and direction of everything that follows. It will be our blessing and mission as we depart. Eucharist, as we said, is who we are and what we do in Christ. We are, at the deepest core and in every fiber and sinew, a eucharistic community.

Communal public worship provides the privileged arena of this sacramental Body of Christ at prayer, whose spiritual geography is multidimensional, for it encompasses the eucharistic, ecclesial, and cosmic boundaries of all human desire for love and meaning and relationship. "O give thanks to the LORD, for he is good, for his steadfast love endures forever" (Ps 136:1). That is the eucharistic promise. However, we cannot always see it, feel it, and taste its sweetness. It is truly *here*, a taste of the kingdom to come, but it is always "not yet" because the times have not as yet grown full, and our sinfulness and alienation and lack of spiritual solidarity veil its gracious activity in our midst. Such half-heartedness affects the Body's wholeness and health. We often lack hope in the promise or lose the desire and willingness to wait eagerly for it in faith and love, unlike those wise maids who kept their flasks of oil replenished and their lamps burning in anticipation of the Bridegroom's arrival for the wedding feast (see Matt 25:4). If it were entirely up to us, our communal lamp may simply go out. Our saving grace is Christ, "God from God, Light from Light," who does not abandon his body.

And so, amid our brokenness and need, faithful assemblies continue to gather. The opening rites at their core are a radical testimony to God's saving acts in Jesus. In gathering, we stubbornly hold out for this hope because some parts of the Body and all of us together have glimpsed its beauty and tasted its sweetness, or we would not continue to pray together "in the name of the Father and of the Son and of the Holy Spirit." The divine invitation is always announced when we do this: "The grace of our Lord Jesus Christ, the love of God, and the communion of the Holy Spirit be with you" is the salutation at the door to this sacramental throne of grace. This proclamation is first and foremost addressed to the whole Body, gathered from the four winds to be the Body, the primary and "singular vessel of devotion." Before any spiritual fruit deepens in the individual woman or man of faith, the arms of "the Spotless Lamb, who is food, table and waiter" for us, as Catherine of Siena muses,[5] lovingly embraces the communal Body that bears his name.

In that invitatory moment, we stand together no longer "I" but "We," and no longer without an identity as an assembly of scattered souls, but as one Body of Christ. In him, our unified identity lives and speaks and unites us in one heart and mind and voice, in praise and thanks to the Father who first uttered that Word of grace and reconciliation in Jesus Christ. St. Paul's kerygmatic words may help to give an image and shape to the true identity of this *singular vessel of devotion* gathered in common prayer: "It is no longer I who live, but it is Christ who lives in me" (Gal 2:20). *Corpus Christi*, Body of Christ, Amen.

The specifically liturgical character of this spiritual geography deserves closer attention in a meditative theology of the assembly at prayer. The esteemed Orthodox theologian of the last century, Alexander Schmemann, described the richness of what Eastern Christians have professed and celebrated for centuries, that is, that the liturgical ritual itself is the manifestation of the "procession" into the heavenly kingdom, an entrance into a "fourth dimension," where all the separations and dualities, the paradigm of the "world" that is passing away, are shed, and together as one Body, we participate in the new reality, the transformed creation.[6] St. Paul's words strike a similar chord in our identity as a sacramental Body:

> You were taught to put away your former way of life, your old self...and to be renewed in the spirit of your minds, and to clothe yourselves with the new self, created according to the likeness of God in true righteousness and holiness.
>
> So then, putting away falsehood, let all of us speak the truth to our neighbors, for we are members of one another. (Eph 4:22–25)

IMAGINING THE SACRAMENTAL BODY AS A SINGULAR VESSEL OF DEVOTION

In an earlier book, *The Holy Preaching* (2000), I explored the nature of the event of proclamation and the preaching of the word within the liturgical assembly and wrestled with the question of how the Catholic sacramental tradition could understand "[Christ] himself who speaks when the holy Scriptures are read in the Church" (SC 7). A subsequent book, *Standing Together in the Community of God: Liturgical Spirituality and the Presence of Christ* (2011), brought the dynamic of relationality and mutuality to bear on the multivalent presence of Christ in the Word proclaimed and preached, in the presider who gathers the community, in the assembly praying and singing, and in the eucharistic gifts of bread and wine. The theological framework was that of *one sacramental presence in four interacting modes*, as articulated in the same paragraph (no. 7) from

Vatican II's *Constitution on the Sacred Liturgy*, which became a guiding dynamic in the reform of the rite in the years that followed.[7] The conclusion of both works is that everything in the liturgy <u>matters</u> and everything <u>forms</u> the sacramental presence. None of these elements are static and individual, but inherently dynamic and communal. When such a communal shift in imagination occurs, I believe a very different, engaged understanding of what is happening in the liturgy unfolds and deepens. <u>Liturgy mystically reveals a divine encounter and event of holy meeting within the gathered Body of Christ.</u> However, such unity is not identified most faithfully by adherence to a precise rubric or approved text, as if it were some encased "thing" that can stand apart from that mutual indwelling. Rather, all elements are integrally relational, dialogical, and participative. The sacramental reality unfolds through the engagement with sacramental signs and symbols that give shape and speak to this unity: *real food* at the common table that is shared and consumed, *presiding voices* that are themselves vulnerable and reflect the complexity and diversity of a shared faith, *participative communities* that reverence the actual bodies that make up her wholeness, and the common *lectio* of a shared biblical tradition passed down, revered, and broken open to utter something new and "fulfilled in your hearing" (Luke 4:21). All this, I suggest, participates in and expresses a "holy communion."

Worshiping out of this relational, dialogical, and participative perspective allows a great spiritual conversation to unfold. Mutual sharing of what is deepest and most precious takes place within the assembly gathered with a living faith and is enhanced by the presider who gathers them and proclaims the Scriptures within the liturgical rhythm of the lectionary and the locus of its revelation in this time and place; all this culminates in the sharing of bread and cup together. The presence of Christ in the eucharistic elements announces this ineffable mystery par excellence, as the documents insist, which is nourishment for the mission to be this Body of Christ in and for the world. The eucharistic species (the blessed sacrament) is inseparable from this event fullness. Building upon the dynamism of the opening invitation to enter the trinitarian communion, receiving Eucharist testifies that the new reality is truly in our midst, a taste of the fullness of grace, and is indeed our sacramental identity, *our* species, as the Spirit-filled, resurrected Body of Christ, Head and members, a holy communion. Christ clings to us and we cling to him. *Corpus Christi*, Body of Christ, Amen.

We proclaim your Death, O Lord,
and profess your Resurrection
until you come again.

THE DEVOTION THAT CHARACTERIZES THIS BODY

Our spiritual tradition has often associated the word *devotion* almost solely within a singular and individual piety. "Devotional exercises" are largely private acts of personal communion with the Lord and disciplined remedies to achieve spiritual health and perfection. Such pieties are well and good and have been exercises of strengthening faith in a variety of cultural and historical milieus. This book, while honoring that, broadens that term to place it in a theologically prior and communal mode, the Church gathered as a "singular vessel of devotion." The appellation comes from the revered sixteenth-century Litany of Loreto, especially popularized at the shrine commemorating the little house of Mary transported by angels to that site in Italy. The idea that Marian piety here is associated so intimately with a dwelling place is appropriate for a reflection upon the sacramental nature of the liturgical assembly as a worshiping Body. The Mother of God is the model of the Church; she is the womb from which life springs; she always has at her center the very Christ she embodies, as numerous icons of the early centuries depict her. In this iconic depiction as ecclesial Mother, Mary is devout with her whole being. With arms spread out in prayer, embodying very much the gesture and posture of the presider at Eucharist, she is fittingly named "Ecclesia Orans," the Church praying.[8]

Hence, it is fitting to play upon the evocative connotation of a "singular vessel of devotion," one of the many images in the Litany. Such poetic speech is a rich and imaginative understanding for the Church praying, the Body in devotion as one, Head and members, and as a eucharistic Body whose whole life and meaning is to name and praise the One who reveals the Father's redeeming love for all generations. "Holy is his name!" we pray. Holy is the Body that bodies forth his name. The sacramental Body at prayer is the dwelling and holy house, like Loreto, of Christ's presence in our midst.

Devotion from this perspective is not extraneous to the liturgy but is an affective expression of the "inexhaustible Mystery" that is the Church's liturgical tradition. It is mystical grace unfolding from the inside out. As one Body with many parts, always united to her Lord who is Head and heart, her devotional acts and attitude of devotion are always *relational, dialogical,* and *participative* in the Trinity's own dynamic communion. There is a synergy of grace whose wellspring is the Spirit of the risen Christ, emanating from the Father's own pierced heart, and circulating in grace-filled energy through the choreography of this Body in every aspect of the rhythm of the liturgical rite. The grace cooperates, as the *Constitution on the Sacred Liturgy* insists, in a poetics that is both human and divine in its essence:

> For the liturgy, "making the work of our redemption a present actuality," most of all in the divine sacrifice of the eucharist, is the outstanding means whereby the faithful may express in their lives and manifest to others the mystery of Christ and the true nature of the Church. (SC 2)

Everything about this dynamic *matters* and everything *forms.* How the assembly embodies the space of worship, how she sings and prays and moves and grows quiet together, is always as an interrelated whole. This is not easy. As for all spiritual disciplines, such forming and acting require exercise and practice, faithful gathering, wise and humble leadership, and a reverence for the symbolic nature of liturgical language and enactment. Such an understanding of communal devotion is important for our times of distracted presence with one another and isolated faith commitments and beliefs. It is a piety of mutual receptivity, soul-centeredness in the Giver of all gifts, and a willing self-emptying, in the manner of Christ, to enter the portal of what the tradition has always called the entrance into the dwelling place of sacramental life: *Domus Dei, Porta Coeli* (House of God, gate of heaven). The sacramental Body at prayer, we could say, is the privileged dwelling place, like the little house of Loreto, a holy house within the house, a "singular vessel of devotion." She is, as the Litany exudes in so many images, a "spiritual vessel, a vessel of honor" and truly a "cause of our joy."

The book has a simple structure, arranged around the interior and exterior dimensions of the liturgical assembly at prayer. Chapter 1 begins with a deepening look at the interiority of the devotional Body and the "attitudes" of mind and heart that shape a Body that clings to Christ and one another. Chapter 2 highlights the choreography of this one Body with its diverse parts, all of which move in rhythm and harmony so that we can truly say that the Body is graceful. Such elements include gesture, posture, reverent attitudes the exterior Body expresses that mirror the reverence within, and the faithful exercise and discipline required for the Body to move in communion. The presider of the assembly plays a key role here. Chapter 3 looks more closely at the voice of the Body, and how she speaks through proclamation and preaching and interceding before God. This voice has a timbre and resonance and its own rhythm that speaks not in a cacophony of voices, but in a richly diverse communal voice that proclaims from the heart of many now gathered as one. Chapter 4 explores the environment and space in which the Body dwells, both interiorly and exteriorly, because the Body is united with the Heart and her own heart beats in communion with him. The actual physical environment in which this can flourish in both dimensions deserves this attention. Finally, a concluding epilogue returns to the heart of the Body's devotedness, our communal heart, the pulse and life of a Body whose trusted heart and center is Christ. Divine holiness is the center of all devotion, as Eucharistic Prayer 3 proclaims:

> You are indeed Holy, O Lord,
> and all you have created
> rightly gives you praise,
> for through your Son, our Lord Jesus Christ,
> by the power and working of the Holy Spirit,
> you give life to all things and make them holy,
> and you never cease to gather a people to yourself,
> so that from the rising of the sun to its setting
> a pure sacrifice may be offered to your name.

There is a pastoral core to everything that will be addressed in these pages. Yet it is also grounded in a systematic tradition that is sacramental, liturgical, and ecclesial in its approach. Together, the pastoral and the systematic work together to uncover the multivalent richness of the people of God, the gift bearers of the treasure in earthenware vessels, holders of a "power [that] belongs to God and does not come from us" (2 Cor 4:7). This ineffable mystery is given distinctive sacramental expression when the assembly comes together in the Lord's name to worship God "in spirit and in truth."

As a meditative theology, the pages that follow attempt to uncover liturgical life from the inside out and build upon the belief that a "felt knowledge" (*sentir*) of a living faith sacramentally expresses itself through an attentive embodiment in rite and in its ritual actors. They attempt to respond to Jesus's question, "What are you looking for?" in the spirit of the disciples' own reply, "Where are you staying?" As we begin this meditative journey, we hear his answer in return, "Come and see."

Writing a book is never the exercise of an individual alone. I am grateful for the many liturgical communities with whom I have been honored to serve and for the many students at both Seattle University's ecumenical School of Theology and Ministry and the lay and religious I teach at the Jesuit School of Theology of Santa Clara in Berkeley, California. My Jesuit community and colleagues in teaching have also supported me by providing a community of brothers and friends in the Lord, including a place apart to write at the Arrupe Jesuit Community at Seattle University and the Della Strada Jesuit Community at Gonzaga University in Spokane. At the Jesuit School of Theology, my colleagues have been supportive and affirming to allow me to complete this work. Barbara Anne Kozee, a graduate assistant generously provided by the school, has proved to be a wise and efficient partner in the final process. My family is also a constant sign to me that the community of faith in which I have thrived has deep roots in them and in their fidelity. Both my family and the Society of Jesus have been a patient and sure vessel in which to grow and to live this vocation of study and service. Thank you. Finally, I am grateful to Donna Crilly, Diane Flynn, and the staff at Paulist Press for providing me the opportunity to share what I believe so deeply about the grace at work when we dare to gather as the Body of Christ to pray in the name of Jesus, in the power of the Spirit, in praise of the Father and giver of all good gifts. And let the people say, "Amen."

ABBREVIATIONS

CSL   Constitution on the Sacred Liturgy, *Sacrosanctum Concilium*

GIRM   General Instruction on the Roman Missal, 3rd edition

LG   *Lumen Gentium*

SC   *Sacrosanctum Concilium*

Chapter 1

"Of the Same Mind, Having the Same Love"

The Devotional Attitude of the Sacramental Body (Phil 2:2)

From on high he flowed like a river,
From Mary he stemmed as from a root,
From the cross he descended as fruit,
As the first-fruit he ascended into heaven
Blessed is his will!

The Word came forth from the Father's bosom,
He put on the body in another bosom;
From one bosom to another did he proceed,
And chaste bosoms are filled with him.
Blessed is he who dwells within us!
St. Ephrem the Syrian, 4th c. (cf. *ST*, 23)

DEVOTION IS AN IDENTIFYING attitude of the liturgical assembly. But as we stated in the introduction, the devotion of the *communio* is not a sum total of individual pieties in the members, extraneous from the worship event, but it is a unifying, sacramental way of being, praying, and acting. Such devotion expresses the living reality of the *totus*

1

Christus, a communal attitude of embodied union through, with, and in Christ and one another. At the same time, the practice of sacramental praying also forms and shapes this devotion and deepens its mark upon the assembly's very soul-in-communion through faithful practice. "Of the same mind, having the same love," of which Paul speaks in Philippians 2:2, originates from Christ—from his mind and his way of loving and being before the Father and the world. The character of this devotion, *per ipsum, et cum ipso, et in ipso*, is *kenotic*, a self-emptying love whose space is really a meeting place, where communion with his Father and those he came to save may be placed. This is where we meet the Lord, are clasped by him, and he clings to us. In the loving and poured out Body of the Lord we have the foundation and contours of our communion, the dwelling place, the holy house, the singular vessel of devotion. Christ's devotion, we could say, is lodged in his own Body. It is a "site," or locus, for communal devotion: The Body of Christ, *Corpus Christi*. When "the hour" for its manifestation in time and space has come (John 17:1), Jesus speaks intimately to his Father about communion, precisely at the time of his most profound self-emptying. He prays not in the isolation of the lonely place apart, but in the intimate setting of the beloved community gathered for the paschal feast:

> Father, I desire that those also, whom you have given to me, may be with me where I am, to see my glory, which you have given me because you loved me before the foundation of the world. (John 17:24)

The ritual gesture of washing the disciples' feet that inaugurates this communion—a tender, albeit humble, task of the servant—scandalizes Peter (John 13:8–9), but this bodily connection as an expression of the kenotic love at the heart of his self-offering is clear and unambiguous on the part of Jesus as he bends before the assembly. This way of being and acting in the world gives flesh and blood to the imagery that follows of the true vine and the branches that cannot abide without him, but literally wither and die (John 15:1–11). It is only later that the dawning of this new communion, the new Body born from the side of the broken Body poured out for them, begins to identify them in turn and shape their mission. Paul will later exclaim that this ecclesial Body of Christ is "the fullness of him who fills all in all" (Eph 1:23). Indeed, in union with Christ and in the power of the Spirit, this Body is now suffused with this trinitarian communion itself, "so that God may be all in all" (1 Cor 15:28).

THE TESTIMONY
OF THE EMBODIED
SACRAMENTAL MOMENT

The eucharistic body and the ecclesial body are always in relationship, as theologians such as Louis Marie Chauvet and Goffredo Boselli and others have insisted.[1] The incarnate Word of God (the "Word of God at the Mercy of the Body") is, at one and the same time, *historical* (lived among us and shared our lot) but also now *crucified and resurrected*, which is a necessary identity of his glorified Body.[2] Sharing in the cross and resurrection of the Lord in the power of the Spirit is where the faithful enter the Body and find their home. The ecclesial Body of Christ, therefore, in all its multidimensions, is a sacramental Body, enfleshed in both the gifts *and* the assembly, and also participates in the life and grace of the glorified Body of the Lord, whose incarnate and historical presence in the world has opened a way for them in his Body. This makes the sacramental Body of Christ now, for us, a "site" and locus of gracious and mutual self-giving. "Let the same mind be in you that was in Christ Jesus," the gathered assembly proclaims. In short, the attitude and contours of this Body are eucharistic and ecclesial, and they are at "the mercy of the Body," to use Chauvet's fruitful insight.

This sense of embodied *place* for the revelation is deepened and handed on in the resurrection and ascension event, because it moves beyond the bounds of time and place. This *now* of the liturgical gathering embraces *all* time and place, a sacramental expression of universality and mission. This is why the postresurrection exhortations are so insistent: "He has been raised; he is not here! Look, there is the place they laid him" (Mark 16:6b), the angel says. It is important to note that the appearances of Jesus all happen where Jesus himself goes out and finds the lost seekers, meeting them on the road and journey of their lives when it now seems that they are without him (i.e., "the appearances"). This meeting of the resurrected Body with the ecclesial Body makes that encounter the place of transformative visitation. The disciples of Jesus are now an apostolic community of faith, summoned, convoked, and called forth, an *ecclesia orans et vivendi*.

Jesus's stern injunction, *Noli me tangere* (John 20:17), amid all these graced encounters, are continued exhortations to see and understand and believe in a new way as the resurrected community gathered in faith. They are asked to let go of what they always thought would be and to respond to what *will be* in Christ as Head and they as members, a "pure grace, pure gift," what L.-M. Chauvet calls a true "conversion."[3] Just as the revelatory "I AM" will be what God will be, so must the members of his Body take on this radical openness to love beyond all telling, shared from the divine heart to the community's heart, spilling over into the heart of the world. Jesus's invitation to "touch the wound" and "eat the breakfast" and "read the story again in a new way so that your hearts burn" are all experiences of being with him, but not their controlling how or why or when that will happen. When we "do this in memory of Him" in our own day, the same is true. These sacramental encounters are always new, in the Spirit.

Christ's resurrection, therefore, is not simply something that happened to him; it is inseparable from what happened to the early disciples and happens now to us. The sacramental Body is the "real presence" of the ecclesial new yeast ("Clean out the old yeast so that *you* may be a new batch" [1 Cor 5:7]). She imagines everything in a new light. For the postresurrection community, Jesus, *as they knew him*, had gone away. But—even more importantly and related to their experience of resurrection faith—the Redeemer and Lord and splendor of the Father was now more present to them in a shared experience of faith than when he walked with them upon the earth. "Behold the old place and old ways and old dispensation," the angel tells the puzzled and frightened women: "Why do you look for the living among the dead?" (Luke 24:5).

Yet, at the same time, Jesus has not simply gone away and left them "orphaned" (John 15:18a). Rather, the angel figure at the tomb comforts them and assures them that "he is going ahead of you to Galilee; there you will see him, just as he told you" (Mark 16:7). "I am coming to you" (John 14:18b) is Jesus's paschal night promise, and he has kept faith. This faith now takes shape in the resurrected dispensation. The sacramental Body of Christ has been born and Christ's sacramental presence is now the mode of intimacy for the beloved community. And so for us. Every assembly that gathers in faith to celebrate the sacred

4

mysteries shares that legacy and that identity. "There you will see him, just as he told you." As Chauvet concludes so poignantly, "And so, we find ourselves in the end sent back to the *body* as the point where God writes God's self in us."[4]

What does all this mean for understanding the interior attitude of the sacramental body at worship? First, Easter visitation and life is not a game of "hide and seek" the resurrected Lord is playing with the community of believers, but a presence *to* them and *with* them and *in* them. This lively presence in faith is on the move, dynamic, and cannot be compartmentalized into an isolated place or moment, cut off from the faith dynamic at work in the Body through the power of the Spirit and animated by Christ as Head of that Body. Because of this, the place and the moment of Christ's promised "real presence" will always be the testimony of a real communion, a participation with Christ before the Father and in the Spirit, a cosmic liturgy that transfigures all places and transforms all time.

Yet, at the same time, the incarnate locus of that testimony is embodied *here* in the specificity of this place, with this gathering of faith. This "here and not yet" reality is a paradox and a struggle for us. We cannot cling to him and yet we must; we cannot touch him, but then, just as he summons Thomas to place his body in the glorified Body, we too must (John 20:27). This is all in the realm of a *mystical reality*[5] (embracing all dimensions and time and place in a spiritual unity) in which the poetic imagination asks us to surrender the logic we know for a truth we cannot stop seeking.

The Body of Christ is knitted together from the inside out, and its outward expression in worship is the truth of a graced communion not of our own making. The Gospel proclamation is embedded in the Body herself.[6] It is realized in the *sentir* ("felt knowledge") of resurrection faith celebrated together. So it is "truly right and just, always and everywhere," as the Eucharistic Prefaces say, that we pause together at key symbolic moments, preeminently in the ritual time of the liturgy, to gather and pray, to give thanks, and to plead for sustenance on that journey toward the fullness of what we know in our sacramental bones is really real and intimately present. As is the case with most poetic logic, one must read the poem and dance the dance and engage the artifact to enter into its mystery. If we do not do this, we simply *are not*, and the whole reason for the life, death, and resurrection of Jesus remains veiled and untapped. The liturgy is that privileged poem and dance and glimpse of beauty.

Second, the Pentecost event signs and seals the Church as the Body of Christ, anoints her with the character and grace of her Lord, and announces precisely *in* her bodiliness the truth of Jesus's words: "And remember, I am with you always, to the end of the age" (Matt 28:20). This is the pilgrim community[7] that is now "the perpetual ordinance" (Exod 12:14). She keeps memory "through him, with him and in him"—distinct but not separate from her Lord, whose paschal mystery she celebrates and announces by her very convocation and coming together. The *sentir* of resurrection faith now extends to a felt knowledge of the assembly's own mind and heart, a convoked identity as "the Church." Where the Body of Christ gathers, the Church is found, and the Lord Jesus is revealed at the center of the assembly as the way, the truth, and the life (John 14:6). The gathering of the Body, therefore, is holy—not for its own sake—but to testify to the universality of the event of redemption and the Love from which it flows. Christ's Body needs a sacramental Body to proclaim this. As L.-M. Chauvet says so pointedly about this, "The body is *the primordial place of every symbolic joining of the 'inside' and the 'outside.'"*[8]

DEVOTION AS AN ATTITUDE OF CHRIST INSCRIBED INTO US

Given this identity of Christ the Head in union with the members as the Spirit-filled resurrected Body of Christ, the *totus Christus*, we return then to the idea of the "attitude of Christ" in our being together, "of the same mind, having the same love" of the Lord. John's Gospel provides a vivid and accessible doorway into this place, which is a symbolic joining of the "inside with the outside." As a revelatory account of the Beloved Disciple concerning his Beloved, we could really call this a "Gospel of sacramental devotion," because it highlights the interiority and single-heartedness of Jesus to his Father, of the Spirit's passion welling up from the depths of his own thirst, and of the disciples' own experience of being grasped by this dynamism.[9] His "attitude" is the icon of our own, and Christ's way of being before the Father and with his beloved gives shape to our mission and identity.

The paschal candle and its many ritual uses demonstrate the trinitarian communion that is now gifted to us. This baptismal seal of identity is engraved and made explicit liturgically and sacramentally when the paschal candle is inscribed at the Easter Vigil, around the primal fire and the assembled believers. Carving the candle, the presider says, "Christ yesterday and today, the Beginning and the End, the Alpha and the Omega: All time belongs to him and all the ages. To him be glory and power through every age and for ever. Amen."[10] The christic identity etched into the candle is the representative sign and symbol of the "attitude" of mind and heart of this sacramental Body. His life, death, and resurrection are embedded into us: "By his holy and glorious wounds," the celebrant continues as the incense grains are placed, "may Christ our Lord guard us and protect us. Amen." This is why the paschal candle now appropriately leads the procession into the holy place, its light lighting all the individual tapers of the worshipers ("The light shines in the darkness, and the darkness did not overcome it" [John 1:5]). It is honored for the great fifty days in a prominent place and finds its home the rest of the year next to the womb and tomb that gave birth and resurrected life to those who are bathed in her waters. Fittingly, it should go to the door of the Church at every funeral to welcome the remains of one of this Body who has now made the great transitus into the full embrace of the Lord she or he served, living now in the new reality of the Communion of Saints around the throne of God. Because we are part of them and they a part of us, their ending always speaks of the beginning, and every act of the assembly is a mirror of the interior attitude that binds her to her Lord. As T. S. Eliot says in "Little Gidding,"

> What we call the beginning is often the end
> And to make an end is to make a beginning.
> The end is where we start from.
> . . . .
>
> We die with the dying:
> See, they depart, and we go with them.
> We are born with the dead:
> See, they return, and bring us with them.
> . . . .

With the drawing of this Love and the voice
 of this Calling

We shall not cease from exploration
And the end of all our exploring
Will be to arrive where we started
And know the place for the first time.

In the gathering, the Pentecostal Church knows who she is, in all places and for all time. This makes her a singular vessel of devotion.

THE ICON OF CHRIST'S DEVOTION: A SHARED LIFE, A GIFTED COMMUNION IN RESPONSE TO A GIFT, A SPACIOUS PLACE FOR A NEW REALITY

Let us look more closely at the devotion of Christ we have been graced to share. The gift of the Father of his own Beloved is where we start if we are to allow ourselves to be gathered into him as one Body: "In the beginning was the Word, and the Word was with God, and the Word was God," John begins (1:1). The Johannine testimony is in many ways a spiritual journal of Jesus's *filial relationship* as the Word of the Father,[11] as *a life to be poured out and shared* ("in him was life"), and *a light that shines in the darkness* of isolation and sin to all who respond to the call and invitation to enter into this embrace. Jesus standing with the Father in a communion of desire, and his relationality in love and for love, is central to this spiritual identity of those who "come and see." The same is true for us. The interior unity of the Body is already taking shape as we enter the house of prayer, for to follow him and to pray in his name is to stand together with him before the Father and to live in generative communion. John's account immediately draws the believer into the story:

From his fullness we have all received, grace upon grace. The law was indeed given through Moses; grace and truth came through Jesus Christ. No one has ever seen God. It is God the only Son, who is close to the Father's heart, who has made him known. (John 1:16–18)

"Closeness to the Father's heart" characterizes the interior place from which Christ acts, a place we have now been given to share and that we receive as a gift. This is the "grace and truth" he communicates to us at the center of our gathering in faith: we share the divine life he lives with his Father. The summoned and convoked Body of Christ, with such a devoted gaze upon the Beloved, so close to the pulse and breath of the Beloved's life, suggests on the assembly's part a call to an *interior attentiveness* that is not first focused upon oneself, but on the relationship of Lover and Beloved. It finds its meaning and life from the *intimacy of loving and being loved.*

To insist again, the Lord's interiority is our icon here. His attitude maps for us the "*symbolic joining of the 'inside' and the 'outside,'*" housed in *the primordial place* of the sacramental Body. What might this look like? We can imagine Christ in communion with his Father, standing with open hands (both receiving and giving the love gift), a posture of dignity and reverence, perhaps even a silence, stillness, and prayerfulness. Could the assembly exteriorly embody this interior disposition and place through a unity of posture and word and quietness together? For the sacramental Body to be such a singular vessel of devotion after Christ's own heart, "of the same mind and having the same love," begins by going to Christ's interior place with him and one another, tapping into that wellspring and river of life whose source is the Father's passion, his "pierced Heart," whose affective union he shares with his Son.

The fecundity of such devoted union is the Spirit's self-gift to the community gathered in the triune name. Individuals let go of the concerns each can only fathom, and they assemble into this shared reality whose space is spacious enough to fathom these concerns. This symbolic joining is a mystical dance, whose rhythm and harmony needs a presider as key to setting this interior attitude.[12] Open hands, a standing together in the trinitarian reality, stillness accompanied by a liberating ownership of "what we have done and what we have failed to do," and trusting that in this gathering Christ is at the heart: this is how the interior attitude slowly emerges and constitutes the sacramental Body. As the hymn "Gather Us In" appropriately proclaims,

> Here in this place new light is streaming,
> Now is the darkness vanished away.
> We see in this space our fears and our dreamings
> Brought here to you in the light of this day.[13]

This is the "tent of mercy" in which we stand together in an emptiness that is not devoid of presence, but, miraculously, bathed in presence. He shares his kenosis with us in the power of the Spirit; in complete surrender and freedom he hands himself over "to be sin who knew no sin, so that in him we might become the righteousness of God" (2 Cor 5:21). And that emptiness is now a space, a place for us to be, with a hunger and a thirst that leads closer to the table where the famished heart is satisfied and communion is celebrated. This is where emptiness is generative and contrition upon the part of the sacramental Body is a conscious turning toward the trinitarian embrace and toward a liberating desire, which is pure gift. This interior attitude is a grace that is risky because it asks that, together, we are here to hand over everything to Christ and allow his attitude to become our own. Systematic theologian Sarah Coakley calls it "desire chastened and purified." In her words,

> For it seems that to step into the realm of the divine, Trinitarian desire, and to seek some form of participation in it through a profound engagement with the Spirit, is both to risk having one's human desires *intensified* in some qualitatively distinct manner, and also to confront a searching and necessary *purgation* of those same human desires in order to be brought into conformity with the divine will.[14]

Longing and hunger are in companionship with conversion, and this engagement is a refashioning that transforms the sacramental Body so that something new emerges in the handing over of one's life to live in the Body together. Before the assembly has heard the word and been convicted by its summons, and prior to her movement to the table, an

10

interior "holy communion" is already taking place. We enter the door of the holy house and in the gathering rites, we know we are home. We are, together, the singular vessel of devotion, poised for mercy, for a fresh word, for a communion that satisfies. The mission of everyday life finds its vibrancy here.

The convoked congregation as an icon of Christ is coming into greater focus. Gathered in the mystery of that abundance, acknowledging its reality as our new sacramental identity, the Body already begins to leave its scattered individualism and to adjust its communal, interior response to a rhythm whose mystical reality is of "the new yeast" and participates in the new reality announced in this time and place. It seems that one cannot "celebrate these sacred mysteries" with any integrity without standing together in this generative emptiness, together and not alone, a Body quiet and present to the Lord who is present to her. It is only then that the presider, who gives voice to the Body's hunger and desire, can cry out in one voice that demands a common response: *"Kyrie eleison, Christe eleison, Kyrie eleison!* May almighty God have mercy on us, forgive us our sins, and bring us to life everlasting. Amen." Christ standing before the Father hands over his own emptiness for us to inhabit as our own holy house. We acknowledge who we are. It is not a static state of being but a place of belonging.

And yet, we must ask, what is the cost of this kenotic identity for the assembly that characterizes this "attitude and mind" of Christ? What is summoned out of her so that she can faithfully celebrate the sacred mysteries entrusted to her as an everlasting covenant? Nothing less than a *conversion of the imagination* must follow upon this acknowledgment of our identity, embodied in this gathering and time and place. But what shape does this take? An example may help at this point. A fellow traveler once shared with me a movement in his prayer that was quite insistent: confronted in so many ways by an intimacy with which the Lord desired to be with him, he found himself almost reluctant to respond, and almost ashamed, because of the paradox of Christ's closeness and the smallness of his own heart to receive it. Even more, how could Christ choose to be so close when there are so many larger and more pressing issues that need redemptive attention? Yet, the Lord did not go away. This was an awesome recognition and a gift of grace.

This pilgrim's journey corresponds to the communal and ecclesial one as well, *a gifted communion in response to a gift.* The invitation to conversion takes the shape of an interior discipline within the Body to let God be God, especially in the arena of gift giving and the willingness to receive the gift. Such a new and disciplined way of being and seeing allows a glimpse into the magnanimous "attitude of Christ"—his mind and his heart: the contours of this dwelling place are so spacious, and there is *always* room. This then is the Christ who summons, gathers, and embraces us:

> Christ Jesus,
> who, though he was in the form of God,
>   did not regard equality with God
>   as something to be exploited,
> but emptied himself,
>   taking the form of a slave,
>   being born in human likeness. (Phil 2:5b–7a)

The kenotic Christ stands before the Father, "full of grace and truth," but not alone and unto himself. He "empties himself" *precisely so he can be with us.* His glory is in sharing the communion he shares in the Trinity's own life, a life that is shared with us. That is his way of glorifying the Father, fulfilling the promise as the Word that was from the beginning with God: "my word...shall not return to me empty," Isaiah announces as the voice of the Lord, "but it shall accomplish that which I purpose" (Isa 55:11). This is the summons and promise God makes to "everyone who thirsts, [to] come to the waters" (v. 1). It is truly a real communion and a holy presence, in him and one another.

If one starts at this heart of it all, the attitude of a real communion and a holy presence gives the Body its sacramental dimensions. And that is always spacious; there is room enough for all, and the Body is richer for its open door and its strong center, as the Lutheran theologian Gordon Lathrop calls this.[15] In a certain way, the expansive attitude of Christ, bodied forth and made present now in us through the practice of our worship, is the truth of Queen Lucy and Lord Digory's interchange with King Tirian in C. S. Lewis's *The Last Battle.* They marvel that the inside of their stable of refuge is truly spacious, like a safe, divine embrace:

> "It seems, then," said Tirian, smiling himself, "that the stable seen from within and the stable seen from without are two different places."

"Yes," said the Lord Digory. "Its inside is bigger than its outside."

"Yes," said Queen Lucy. "In our world too, a stable once had something inside it that was bigger than our whole world." It was the first time she had spoken, and from the thrill in her voice, Tirian now knew why. She was drinking everything in even more deeply than the others. She had been too happy to speak.[16]

As for Lucy, the same holds for the sacramental Body. The felt knowledge and awesome wonder at the heart of eucharistic praise and thanksgiving come about by experiencing and participating in a new reality, in taking on a new attitude that organically emerges from "drinking everything in even more deeply." There are no words to describe this awe except to acknowledge, as every Eucharistic Prayer begins, that

> it is truly right and just, our duty and our salvation,
> always and everywhere to give you thanks,
> Lord, holy Father, almighty and eternal God,
> through Christ our Lord.[17]

If we take seriously the sacramental Body as a privileged singular vessel of devotion—the wellspring and abode for any individual affectivity and desire—we begin to see that Christ's communion with his Father and the Spirit's love overflowing as this love between the Father and the Son also shapes the contours of our sacramental identity as the Body of Christ. In this transformed interiority, we begin to taste and see and know that the Lord Jesus clings to us and we cling to him; we are caught up in the trinitarian awe, reverence, stillness, spaciousness, and attentiveness to the other so that it becomes our christic attitude together. Inseparable from this attitude is our unity with and devotion to our sisters and brothers who, in our ecclesial bond, announce in one voice that "the hour has come" for the limbs of this Body to claim their common interiority as "true worshipers [who] worship the Father in spirit and in truth, for the Father seeks such as these to worship him" (John 4:23). It is how we then live and pray and intercede. In short, the shape of the singular vessel of devotion begins inside.

THE ICON OF LORD JESUS AS THE CRUCIFIED ONE: AN ESSENTIAL DEVOTIONAL ATTITUDE OF THE SACRAMENTAL BODY

As we said earlier, the sacramental and ecclesial Body is born in the resurrection/Pentecost event. But the doorway into that new reality is in the shape of a cross.[18] The glorified Lord, we said, necessarily embraces his crucified and resurrected reality. The wounds Christ bears are glorious wounds, but they do not disappear with the empty tomb. They are a sign of the victory and a testimony to the saving acts of God on Jesus's behalf. In the Easter appearance in the locked room, "Jesus came and stood among them and said, 'Peace be with you.' After he said this, he showed them his hand and his side" (John 20:19b–20). These signs are the "way of the cross" traced upon Jesus's own Body. They are inscribed into him "out of the same mind, and his having the same love" that pierced his own Father's heart. They are a *primordial place* and express the *symbolic joining of the 'inside' and the 'outside'* in Christ's Body, to use Chauvet's words.[19] The cross, then, functions as the divining rod of the trinitarian locus for the saving acts flowing from Christ's own heart. This impelling Spirit within the members seeks his sacramental grace and presence in the places of deepest emptiness, alienation, and sin, both in their midst and in all creation, in order to embrace and redeem these wounds and consecrate them as "glorious wounds." This is how Christ's interior attitude opens up the spacious place in which we gather. As the great Corrie ten Boom spoke so prophetically, "There is no pit so deep, that God's love is not deeper still."[20]

Where humanity longs for wholeness and her crosses are all too apparent, there is Christ, sent by the Father as Beloved in this radical way of love, and there is the generative Spirit of communion with all who seek nourishment at this well of all desire. So the liturgy, as incarnate locus of this interior reality, always begins with this stunning cosmic reality: "In the name of the Father, and of the Son, and of the Holy Spirit." We respond in affirmation: "Amen. So be it."

This affirmation to cling to Christ and let him cling to the Body signifies this same cruciform way and truth and life. "Of the same mind

14

and having the same love" suggests that the sacramental Body's own wounds and the crosses she bears are also a part of that iconic identity inscribed into her christic body as an interior attitude of devotion. The First Letter to Peter speaks eloquently of this:

> For to this you have been called, because Christ also suffered for you, leaving you an example, so that you should follow in his steps....He himself bore our sins in his body on the cross, so that, free from sins, we might live for righteousness; by his wounds you have been healed. (1 Pet 2:21, 24)

The wounds in his body are handed over on the cross and this is the liberating pattern for us, the pathway to our place of healing, and the ritual inscribing of the new reality into us, "one Body, one Spirit in Christ."[21] So it is important to see how the cross is the doorway into this interior attitude of the crucified and risen Christ into which the sacramental Body is being formed. Only from that interior center, gathered to her Lord, can she make the procession out for the ritual testimony the sacramental Body claims at word and table. This is the shape of the Body's self-offering in union with her Lord. This is the shape of a holy communion.

THE SACRAMENTAL BODY PRAYING: WHERE THE INSIDE AND THE OUTSIDE COALESCE

The liturgical imagination helps when considering this interior refashioning taking place in the assembly at prayer. We return for an example to our own sacramental beginnings, embodied in the great events of Easter and the pillar of fire that leads the people out of slavery into freedom. "Christ our Light" is now our standard bearer, born from the great fire to light all the many fires that come together in the Body. It is no accident that on this night of great joy, the paschal candle is inscribed with the form of a cross, and the incense wounds lavishly decorate the candle's body.[22] They are the victorious signs that point to both cross and empty tomb. Cross and glorified wounds unite us to him, body and soul. This is why the assembly sings at the Adoration of the Cross in the Good Friday Liturgy of the Passion,

> Sweet the timber, sweet the iron,
> Sweet the burden that they bear!

And in a poetic conceit that upsets the common expectation of God's way of turning the world's defeat into a sweet moment of intimacy, the cross becomes the fertile marriage bed of heaven and earth in a profound way. As the hymn goes on to proclaim,

> Lofty timber, smooth your roughness,
> Flex your boughs for blossoming;
> Let your fibers lose their toughness,
> Gently let your tendrils cling;
> Lay aside your native gruffness,
> Clasp the body of your King!

So the sign of the cross embedded in the paschal candle is "an outward sign of an interior reality," to use the traditional sacramental terminology. It connotes a heart and a mind whose outward reality are the horizontal and vertical beams that stretch "from the rising of the sun to its setting" (EP 3; Mal 1:11) and also bring together earth and heaven. It unites the heavenly and the earthly liturgy (SC 8) and "gathers the nations into the peace of God's Kingdom"[23] and, at the same time, descend and anchor themselves deep into the earth and the nether regions, only to ascend from there to the sky and the light and the heights of heaven, where "Christ is seated at the right hand of the Father to intercede for us."[24] The cruciform dimensions of the mystical communion have been gathered up within the liturgical gathering. Its diverse members reflect how spacious the holy house is, and where the Body of Christ lives. In sacramental terms, this assembly "bodies forth" Christ as the center of all reality, as gatherer and anchor and vulnerable lover. "Gently let your tendrils cling," we sing as we sign ourselves. "Clasp the body of your King." Sharing in the cross and resurrection of the Lord in the power of the Spirit is the attitude of Christ in which we are inscribed, and the way of the cross prepares the Body for the resurrected reality she shares in the power of the Spirit, as a Body united as Head and members in holy communion. We stand in

16

that Easter place every Sunday. The presider gathers the Body into holy communion. We are praying in the name of Jesus and in the power of the Holy Spirit.

To sum up the rich dimensions of this cruciform doorway within attentive liturgical practice: the words and gestures we use to enter into this sacred gathering, "In the name of the Father, and of the Son, and of the Holy Spirit," suggest more than a talisman or spiritual moniker. The assembly is not "dropping names" here in order to assert her importance. Rather, to pray in this name is to enter into that trinitarian communion where the Body's "human desires are *intensified* in some qualitatively distinct manner," as Coakley speaks of this trinitarian embrace. It also risks "to confront a searching and necessary *purgation* of those same human desires in order to be brought into conformity with the divine will."[25] The interior and exterior coalesce. "Amen," we say, to that.

SOME FINAL REFLECTIONS ON CORPOREAL INTERIORITY AND THE SACRAMENTAL BODY

It is important to note that although this interior attitude of the crucified Lord Jesus is essential to the deepening corporate identity embodied by worshipers in the liturgy as they understand their identity together, it is also inseparable from and shapes the formation that occurs within the exterior ritual practice of worship itself. Praying, as the tradition asserts, shapes believing. Just as the Vatican document on the liturgy speaks paradoxically of the liturgy as both "fount and summit of Christian life" (SC 10), the interiority of the Body nurtures the outward expression and is itself *intensified* by means of that very enactment. This is the mutuality of grace that flows from "the inside to the outside" and back again in mutual receptivity. The formation of the singular vessel of devotion does not simply follow a linear progression from inner attentiveness to exterior expression, but dances in a cyclic rhythm, where each enriches the other and there is a spiral of increasing intensification toward greater union between Head and members.

Once again, Chauvet's observation makes even more sense regarding this interplay between attitude and expression, interior attentiveness and faithful enactment: "The body is *the primordial place of every symbolic joining of the 'inside' and the 'outside.'*"[26] Because of the incarnate reality of the sacramental Body—no mere idealized or imaginary communion—an interior attitude and configuration to the mind and heart of Christ needs a body to be a sacramental Body, as Chauvet has also remarked. He insists that "faith cannot be lived in any other way, including what is most spiritual in it, than *in the mediation of the body*, the body of a society, of a desire, of a tradition, of a history, of an institution, and so on. What is most spiritual takes place in the most corporeal." Hence, the whole sacramental economy and the faith that is its "fount and summit" is always a relational exchange and a mutuality in the communication of desire, whose conduit for us is "at the mercy of the body" in all its dimensions.[27]

One could thus raise the legitimate issue of whether communal, interior devotion can ever be possible without a concrete practice of praying *together*, of the community hearing the summons of God's desire and the purification that accompanies it, and the sharing of this holy communion that moves inevitably toward some sense of corporate *mission* that flows from the celebration. In this ritual and ecclesial vacuum, is it even possible for formators charged with sacramental preparation to communicate the depth of the liturgical experience to those who never practice and enter into the embrace of the sacramental Body of the liturgical assembly? As theologian David Fagerberg has noted, "Mystery is not something to know, it is something to be and do."[28]

Sacramental life and the sacramental Body are ecclesial vessels of devotion. Christians who claim identity in the Body of Christ but eschew a concrete commitment to sacramental practice, or those who incorporate their own individualized versions of Christian rituals divorced from the Body, present grave challenges to integrating an ever-deepening union of life and mission with Christ within the *ekklesia*, specifically "the Church-as-body," as Chauvet calls the liturgical "epiphany."[29] The living Church as a Spirit-filled resurrected Body of Christ provides the primordial locus for the sacramental presence of Christ, crucified and risen, glorious Lord and intimate companion. That "real presence" can only have a name and a face when communicated ritually, in sacred space and time, always an eventful interchange that is "relational, dialogical, and participative."[30] No catechism description can ever adequately form an attitude "of the same mind, [and] sharing the same love" when it is disembodied from faithful liturgical practice in community on a consistent basis.

Any body needs exercise to function in a holistic manner. This is no less true for the singular vessel of devotion, a liturgical assembly actively praying as one heart and mind and voice (see Rom 15:6).[31] She can only be "the Word of God at the mercy of the Body," because the concrete gathering of the holy people of God houses the sacramental locus and site of the presence of Christ. Only as this praying vessel can she breathe deeply to utter a voice to sing God's praise and be "the outstanding means whereby the faithful may express in their lives and manifest to others the mystery of Christ and the true nature of the Church" (SC 2). There is no other way than the bodily, sensual way, despite our efforts to idealize holy communion and interior surrender to Christ, he in us and we in him.

Let the heavens praise your wonders, O LORD,
  your faithfulness in the assembly of the holy ones. (Ps 89:5)

The chasm created when the interior attitude is not nourished in exterior practice can penetrate deeper levels in the human and communal soul that may not be immediately conscious. If one has no ecclesial Christian identity expressed in some ritual language of prayer, can someone enter into the lush symbolic and eucharistic dimensions of "the ineffable Mystery," of which sacramental life is an iconic doorway? Is this source of nourishment accessible in another way, God willing? Or, on the other hand, what happens when the sacramental richness a liturgical community offers is stunted and merely self-focused? Such limited liturgical horizons can cause the Body to atrophy, unable to reach beyond the bounds of its own safe environs to seek out and embrace the disaffected, the marginalized, and the uncatechized people of today, particularly the young who have no sacramental foundation to their "spiritual but not religious" self-identity?

Much is at stake here. The gift of sacramental grace requires a willing body to receive it, precisely *as* gift (and not a possession), and to respond in a similar christic pattern.[32] Chauvet describes the necessity of this gift-reception-return dynamic as the symbolic interchange of *gratuitousness* and *graciousness*, the mode in which "one can approach the mystery of communication between God and humanity." Even more, our relationship with Christ and one another "is inscribed [in the body] *in* this exchange"; it both structures our Christian identity and is the language of that intimacy and the bearer of its grace.[33]

The kerygmatic restlessness of being "broken and poured out for the life of the world" finds its original language in the dynamism Christ shares with the members of his Body. Sacramental communion in response to the trinitarian embrace is quintessentially a communion with a people who discover their truest personal identity in handing over themselves to the divine Other—to a God who then disperses this communion through the assembly of sisters and brothers in Christ "praying and singing" next to them (SC 7), persons often not of their own choosing. It moves outside the door of this tent of meeting "to all who seek him with a sincere heart." This is the creative tension of a sacramental Body needing both a sure identity and also a wide arm of embrace. True worship, as Gordon Lathrop insists, is "an open door" but still needs "a strong center."[34] Dancing in rhythm with this delicate balance and communicating the significance of this ambiguity is a profound dilemma in contemporary ecclesial and secular life. Regular worship practice is the vessel's ongoing faith formation and the integral exercise of her limbs, so that she might be a living body of faith for all. But such challenges necessitate that the Body stretch and strengthen these limbs.

Despite the real challenges, we know in faith that grace is already at work, because hearts are being stirred, the longing is real, and the originating desire of God to share the perichoretic dance with the Beloved is insatiable. As a consequence of this original blessing, the "inside" of many hearts who have lost the liturgical memory still pines for some "outside" sense of belonging and covenant commitment. In the christic attitude of the Church at prayer, she is always attentive to those who experience themselves on the margins of or outside the communal vessel of devotion. She finds new ways to allow the seeking ones to sense the liberating and joyous possibility such "clinging to Christ and one another" offers, which is, to use Fagerberg's terms, "a doing and a being" and not first dogmatic knowledge set in stone. This puts even more responsibility on the sacramental Body to be that "strong center and open door" that is always ready and always eager *to invite and to gather* everyone into this tent of meeting.[35]

There is no way around this living tension: the sacramental Body's hunger for union with her Lord is inseparable from her own longing and willingness *to receive* the searching soul and those who feel excluded or alienated from that communion. Jesus's own interior attitude shared with the disciples in Luke must be a shared experience of the gathered community always and in every place:

> When the hour came, he took his place at the table, and the apostles with him. He said to them, "I have eagerly desired to eat this Passover with you before I suffer; for I tell you, I will not eat it until it is fulfilled in the kingdom of God." (Luke 22:14–16)

The ecclesial Body of Christ is always truly hungry herself, in union with Christ's own longing to share the meal with the beloved and "to gather your children together as a hen gathers her brood under her wings" (Matt 23:37). The communion banquet is not simply satisfying the local assembly's desire for union with Christ, their Head. The hunger is intrinsically outward looking, a willingness to gather in and make the circle wider, more diverse, more whole. For the *totus Christus*, "the person of Christ and also this collective 'body of Christ,'" Chauvet again notes,

> Differences are no longer partitions; on the contrary, they offer to the "body of Christ" this rich diversity of members and functions which any body needs. The other is no longer considered a rival or potential enemy, especially on a religious plane; the other must be welcomed as a brother or sister.[36]

This is the "already and not yet character" of this dynamism we call the sacramental Body. Her icon is the self-emptying Lord Jesus. Her receptivity to God, in the transforming Spirit who consecrates and makes all things new, immediately invites her into a receptivity toward all those for whom Christ's crucified and risen Body now awaits in glory. She desires those others to come to know the joy she has found in this "temple of his body" (John 2:21), and, at the same time, she acknowledges her need to make the spacious house a dwelling for all who come. This requires an interior discipline and a spiritual practice that continually asks conversion on her part, what Coakley called "the *purgation*

21

of those desires in order to be brought into conformity with the divine will."[37] This is part of "having the same mind and heart" of Christ.

AN INSIDE THAT SPILLS OVER INTO THE OUTSIDE

Further chapters will address the "already and not yet" contours of this singular vessel of devotion and its exterior expression in the ways the sacramental Body ritualizes in practice, gives voice, and inhabits the space in which the gathered Body of Christ cooperates with this "strong center and open door" interiority. Acknowledging any lack of spaciousness by a liberating recognition of her own need for conversion, she always must turn toward the desire that first called her and the summons to "come and see," in which the sacramental and ecclesial reality was called into being. To trust in that and not to close off what God is doing in a world that finds corporate worship increasingly peripheral is also an issue of this corporeal interiority that is in consort with the attitude of Christ.

This interior exploration can now provide the foundation for a closer look at the exterior contours of the singular vessel of devotion, as she bodies forth her reality and identity and communion in the Body of Christ. Since "matter and form" constitute the outward sign of this sacramental reality, we will discover in the next chapters that everything *matters* and everything *forms*, and the Body's intentionality and attentiveness to these aspects allows the rhythm and harmony of the sacramental Body to dance with grace and to deepen her communion with Christ and one another. In the end, *devotio* is a singular and profound dedication to the Other and to the Body's participation in that communion that flows from the Trinity's own way of being. Classic understanding of *devotional acts* always includes "a solemn or formal act" to testify to this interior orientation.[38] The liturgical assembly at prayer is that eventful action that announces the Church as that "visible society and spiritual communion" that is "one complex reality"[39] embodying the symbolic joining of what is most human and divine in the Body of Christ.

22

As *Lumen Gentium* clarified the sacramental nature of the Church and Walter Kasper emphasized in his ecclesiological writing,

> The Church, on the one hand, proceeds totally from Christ and is always turned toward him, and on the other hand is completely a sign and instrument for service to human beings and to the world. This concept is especially well-suited for relating and differentiating, in a nuanced way, the visible structure and spiritual essence of the Church.[40]

Devotional acts by the Body communicate the covenantal sign and symbol that both express and effect what Kasper calls this "spiritual essence," which we call here an interior union of Head and members. She stands at the crossroad of what Henri de Lubac has termed "a matrix of symbolic relationships."[41] The sacred liturgy is a privileged proclamation and moment of that testimony of God's saving acts in Jesus in our midst. The assembly at prayer and at any time and place embraces that eschatological tension and herself relies upon the fullness to come, which can only proceed from God's initiative. She clings to her Lord, and trusts that, although pilgrims in a strange land (Heb 11:13–16), the communion she shares as his Body and always united to her Head will effect that glorious future, through the indwelling of the Holy Spirit at the heart of her being. As *Lumen Gentium* attests,

> In order that we might be unceasingly renewed in him [see Eph 4:23], (Christ) has shared with us his Spirit who, *being one and the same in head and members*, gives life to, unifies and moves the whole body. Consequently, his work could be compared...to the function that the principle of life, the soul, fulfills in the human body.[42]

That utter reliance on the dynamism of the Spirit, which is the very gift of grace that unites her as one Body in him, constitutes the "soul" of this sacramental Body. Inside animates the outside, an incarnational whole.

The trinitarian communion now has a shape in the world, a matter and form that has gestures and movements and a voice and a space in which this "one complex reality" is, in a matrix of symbolic relationships,[43] *Corpus Christi, corpus verum*, and *corpus mysticum*, distinct realities that are inseparable from one another. That is the nature of real communion with a holy presence. In the next chapter, we move to the exterior "shape" of this Body and ponder whether attentiveness to these sensible features of the singular vessel of devotion within the celebration of the liturgy can be said, in truth, to be the sign and symbol that "effects the reality that she signifies" when its matter and form are honored and given full embodiment and expression. The sacramental economy asks no less from the Church gathered in this "summit toward which the full activity of the Church is directed (and) at the same time…the fount from which all the Church's power flows" (SC 10). As Paul says in Colossians, the primal stuff of this Body is Christ, the *totus Christus*, and she belongs to him and "holds fast to the head." The Head of the Body is the source and wellspring, "from whom the whole body, nourished and held together by its ligaments and sinews, grows with a growth that is from God" (2:19). We move now from the "inside" to the "outside," knowing that this gracious exchange with the Lord of all our longing is a real, sensual, and living encounter, as Augustine said so poetically, with a "beauty ever ancient, ever new."[44]

Chapter 2

THE MOVEMENT OF THE TRUE BODY AND THE MYSTICAL BODY

Communion Incarnate

> In the catacombs, the most frequent image is the figure
> of a woman in prayer, the *Orant*; she represents the one
> true attitude of the human soul. It is not enough to say
> prayers; one must become, *be* prayer, prayer incarnate. It
> is not enough to have moments of praise. All of life, each
> act, every gesture, even the smile of the human face, must
> become a hymn of adoration, an offering, a prayer. One
> should offer not what one has, but what one is.
>
> Paul Evdokimov, *The Sacrament of Love:*
> *The Nuptial Mystery in the Light of the Orthodox Tradition*[1]

THE EXPLORATION, AS WE said at the end of the last chapter, now
moves to the vessel of devotion as embodied sacramental matter and
form. We will highlight the choreography of this one Body with its
diverse parts, all of which move in rhythm and harmony, so that we can
truly say that the sacramental Body is graceful and "full of grace." Such
elements include gesture, posture, reverent attitudes of the exterior

body that mirror the reverence within, and the exercise and discipline required for the Body to move in communion. We will also look at the role of liturgical leadership in helping this assembly to pray as one Body and not a muster of isolated pieties. In this intentional communion, the Holy Spirit, "being one and the same in head and members" (LG 7) begins the movement from the inside to the outside, to breathe life into the Body and provide the resonance that will echo through the assembly, who has gathered "in the Name of the Father, and of the Son, and of the Holy Spirit." Fifteenth-century poet Bianco da Siena puts that movement into words that are sung now when Christians gather in the power of the Spirit that makes them one in Christ and one another. The soul, imagined in communal song as that which "gives life to, unifies and moves the whole body" (LG 7), begs to share in the very ardor of "Love Divine." The assembly sings,

> O let it freely burn,
> Till earthly passions turn
> To dust and ashes in its heat consuming;
> And let your glorious light
> Shine ever on my sight,
> And clothe me round, the while my path illumining.
>
> And so the yearning strong,
> With which the soul will long,
> Shall far out pass the power of human telling;
> For none can guess its grace,
> Till love creates the space
> Wherein the Holy Spirit makes its dwelling.[2]

A concrete experience of such communal indwelling given expression in the body may provide a way into this discussion.

I once had the good fortune to be at the Benedictine Abbey of Our Lady of Montserrat in Spain on June 24, the Feast of St. John the Baptist, the patron of all Catalonia. The monastery itself had been an important preserver of Catalan language and customs, especially during the Franco regime. So the sentiment for a communal identity is strong. After evening prayer in the beautiful abbey church, where the shrine of Our Lady of Montserrat is the vigilant icon of this monastic singular vessel of devotion, the community then processed to the outside of the church. In the darkness, the monks and their guests circled around a large fire blazing in the plaza. From this lofty viewpoint, one could see a troupe of torches in the night, moving up the steep mountain road to the abbey from the town and valley far below. The torchbearers were all young people running to join the monastic community, to join their pilgrim torches to the abbey's great fire. The two communities merged and something mystical and wonderful happened. They locked arms around one another's shoulders and began to dance a Catalan step around the fire, while singing a cultic song. It was a ritual of remembrance and deep symbolic identity for this community, in which the whole is infinitely greater than the sum of her parts. Communion and holy presence can never be separated. This deep sacramental truth radiated in and through this circular dance of devotion.

The significance of this communal ritual and song for this discussion is that the individual bodies of these two groups, joined together intentionally around the fire and sharing ritual movement and song at a special time and in a special place, was an epiphany of presence, rooted in the one body together. There was no liturgy committee who prepared this from the top down, prescribing specific rubrics and thereby instructing the assembled body what to do. The spiritual direction of this outward expression of faith rose up from the soul of the communal body, which could not have been understood in its fullness by each one alone. Rather, this singular vessel of devotion expressed the "symbolic joining of the inside to the outside" in the context of the Church's evening prayer, whose spacious tent had made the meeting place and the gathered body expansive and richer, what we called earlier a "strong center and an open door." To witness this sacramental Body form in the darkness and to see its common gestures and unity around this primal symbol that spans both Christian and Catalan origins was to witness the power of the worshiping assembly to be a sign and a symbol much greater than their individual selves, a glimpse at the communion of Christ with his Church, the Bridegroom with the bride, God and God's creation, and all a part of the Trinity in communion with one another.

The "communion incarnate" at Montserrat was the crossroads of this matrix of symbolic relationships of which de Lubac so often commented.[3] It announced a covenantal truth in the particularity of feast and community and the radiance of the season in its pilgrimage toward the light. And the enduring truth is this: the perennial faithfulness of God with us, the members of this Body who receive this gift and are united together throughout the cosmos, saved and redeemed by Christ, convoked and summoned through the indwelling power of the Spirit. Indeed, de Lubac argues that the milieu of these relationships of personal, sacramental, and ecclesial bodies should be "intentionally ambiguous," and this is itself "significant," which means that *the ambiguity itself* bears an essential role in communicating and bodying forth the mode of presence in which the sacramental reality is expressed. God initiates the graceful dance. This affirms the notion that liturgical poetics is a fit mode of expression for a mystery that cannot be grasped first and foremost by our own systematized categories of holiness as simply *here* and not *there*. The Ascension Preface sings of this mystery in the true and mystical Body:

> It is truly right and just, our duty and our salvation,
> always and everywhere to give you thanks,
> Lord, Holy Father, almighty and eternal God,
> through Christ our Lord.
>
> For after his Resurrection
> he plainly appeared to all his disciples
> and was taken up to heaven in their sight,
> that he might make us sharers in his divinity.
>
> Therefore, overcome with paschal joy,
> every land, every people exults in your praise
> and even the heavenly Powers, with the angelic hosts,
> sing together the unending hymn of your glory....[4]

The exultant dance and rhythm of the sacramental Body at prayer allow the grace to flow through the gathering, where something new is always being born in and through the Spirit. This Spirit-filled, resurrected identity of Christ both resides in the Body and is utterly free of the limitations of the assembly that embodies her, individually or even collectively. It is both the "font" from which the Spirit is given as pure gift and as "sweet anointing from above," to echo the poetic Pentecost hymn, as well as the "summit" expression of her union with Christ, the true *totus Christus*. The wholeness of the sacramental Body at prayer holds this treasure as one, as simultaneously as she is being held in one tender embrace. This is the theological understanding of the *communio* and the *koinonia* who by nature is a "sharing together" and a participation in a baptismal identity and life shaped by a common covenantal bond, Christ Jesus, who is this "communion incarnate." As Jesus spoke to Nicodemus about the new life the kingdom of God offers,

> What is born of the flesh is flesh, and what is born of the Spirit is spirit. Do not be astonished that I said to you, "You must be born from above." The wind blows where it chooses, and you hear the sound of it, but you do not know where it comes from or where it goes. So it is with everyone born of the Spirit. (John 3:6–8)

This pneumatological foundation gives the sacramental Body her cohesion and weaves the sinews of her limbs into a true body that is a mystical Body—one, holy, catholic, and apostolic. As *Lumen Gentium* 4 says, "The Spirit dwells in the Church and in the hearts of the faithful, as in a temple (cf. 1 Cor 3:16; 6:19)." Being "born again" in the Spirit is not one's individual spiritual achievement, but always a participation in the living union with Christ and one another. "Hence the universal Church," LG 4 continues, citing a number of patristic sources, "is seen to be 'a people brought into unity from the unity of the Father, the Son, and the Holy Spirit.'" The concrete assembly *matters* and how she dances is the *form* that matters, as we will highlight further on. Liturgy, particularly in the Eucharist par excellence, is not the static idea of this, but the event of its testimony.

De Lubac notes in another important essay, entitled "Christian Community and Sacramental Communion,"[5] that the relational identities expressed in the Body of Christ are *distinct* but never *separate*. In fact, in a rather bold and yet traditional patristic understanding of this communion of the Corpus Christi as "true Body and Mystical Body," de Lubac asserts that any notion of real presence in the sacramental elements can only *be* because of its prior expression within the true nature of the Church, which is Christ as Head united to the limbs of his ecclesial Body. The ecclesial, sacramental liturgy is the privileged moment of this. Arguing with copious reference to these early sources, de Lubac illumines for us how sharing in the Eucharist is the testimony of "two simultaneous things that make one whole," rather than the description of "two successive objects." "*This* is my Body," seen from this perspective, takes on a fecund significance. The ecclesial Body must always

29

be seen in relational communion with the eucharistic species and the Lord she announces, whose crucified, resurrected, and glorified Body is the One sent by the Father, the gift given in whom we "live and move and have our being,"[6] and "we too are his offspring" (Acts 17:28), formed in the same mind and sharing in the same love. He goes further:

> For the body of Christ that is the Church is in no way *other* than the body and blood of the mystery....Through the Eucharist each person is truly placed within the one Body. It unites all the members of it among themselves, as it unites them with their one head....In this way, little by little, the *"whole Christ"* comes into being, who is always in our minds the ultimate end of the mystery.[7]

The liturgical assembly is the privileged expression of the unity of the Church and manifests the mystery of Christ with a clarity that transcends any doctrine about Christ; this exposes the poverty of any notion of the "true Body" (*corpus verum*) of Christ as limited to the sacramental elements alone and somehow existing both distinctly and separately from the sacramental Body that gathers in praise and thanks.[8] As de Lubac insists in pursuing his point of the intentional and significant ambiguity about who and what the *Corpus Christi* is, he says,

> Is the Church not the continuation of Christ? *Christ is trans-ferred to the Church*: these simple words are pregnant with significance. And the passing of Christ into his Church was itself prepared, or even prefigured by an earlier passing, that of the Church into Christ: is the Church not the greater body from which Christ drew his body?[9]

This provides much fruit for reflection, when we begin to see this "crossroads" of the sacramental Body—such as happened on that evening in Montserrat—as a moment of testimony of real presence, a new Passover embodied, precisely when she acts as a Body in unity of body, mind, and spirit. Christ "draws his body" now from this sacramental Body. Whatever personal pieties and devotion each member of the assembly carries within herself, she lays aside this focus on personal illumination, sweet and uplifting as it is, in order to hand it over to the rhythm and harmony of the Body in liturgical prayer. For Christ is not only in us, but we are all, now and together, in Christ. And so each believer need not fear that she will lose something in order to enter into the self-emptying of Christ in the wholeness of the event. Indeed, the rich treasure, manifested in "clay jars" (2 Cor 4:7), enriches each within the whole, because he first emptied himself, "being born in human likeness…and being found in human form" (Phil 2:7). The kenotic "we" is God's way of holy communion, as 2 Corinthians goes on to say, "so that it may be made clear that this extraordinary power belongs to God and does not come from us." Paul goes on to say, "For while we live, we are always being given up to death for Jesus' sake, so that the life of Jesus may be made visible in our mortal flesh. So death is at work in us, but life in you" (2 Cor 4:11–12). Once again, the power and richness of "*This* is my Body" should engender a devotion in the sacramental Body that is expressed and "made visible in our mortal flesh." It is signed and sealed in a profound act of dedication. This is the privileged grace of gathering in sacramental communion in which the Body clings to Christ and Christ clings to her. As Preface 1 of Sundays in Ordinary Time sings, this is why we gather, why it is "truly right and just, our duty and our salvation," to offer praise and thanks in union with Christ in one voice in exultant acclamation:

> For through his Paschal Mystery,
> [Christ] accomplished the marvelous deed,
> by which he freed us from the yoke of sin and death,
> summoning us to the glory of being now called
> a chosen race, a royal priesthood,
> a holy nation, a people for your possession,
> to proclaim everywhere your mighty works,
> for you have called us out of darkness
> into your own wonderful light.

Images of movement, such as "called into this wonderful light" as "God's intimate possession," and "summoned now to be a priestly body, after the mind and heart of Christ" begin to offer the contours of this sacramental Body and the expression of her devotion. What might that look like for us? How do the movements and gestures, the choreography of ritual, and the silence of shared awe embody this shape more faithfully, so that we can be that iconic doorway into the mystery in which we are embraced, and not simply a self-expression of each one's desire? As simple as it sounds, the answer is the intentional quality of the *matter* and the *form* this sacramental expression of the Body of Christ at prayer enacts, where the outside expresses the inside, and where the "true Body and the Mystical Body" expresses its identity and gracefulness in a manner that "proclaims the mighty works of God" who gathers us in unity, rather than one that watches the sacred mysteries from the distinct and separate pews of each one's private devotions. After exploring these concrete expressions, we will end by returning to the importance of "intentional ambiguity" in these movements that not only allows but sets in motion the Holy Spirit's hallowing to move in and through the Body with a grace that is graceful.

HOW THE BODY MANIFESTS THE BODY: SOME PRACTICAL LITURGICAL PRINCIPLES FOR THE "SINGULAR VESSEL OF DEVOTION"

The wisdom of Louis-Marie Chauvet may help to anchor this very practical discussion. He says quite forcefully, regarding the assembly as a scandalous but necessary vehicle of sacramental presence,

> "It is great, the mystery of faith!" Before it applies to the Eucharist, this expression applies to the concrete assembly as church. Here there is both mystery and scandal. This is what is not self-explanatory, and for the believing intelligence the scandal of the presence of Christ in the Eucharist risks serving as a mock scandal (that is, merely intellectual) if one ignores this primary scandal, an existential one: the encounter of the living Christ which is possible only through the mediation of a church, indeed holy but composed of sinners, indeed body of Christ but made up of divided members, indeed temple of the Holy Spirit but so parsimoniously missionary. The concrete assembly of every

single Sunday confronts Christians with the harsh reality of this mediation that everyone seeks to forget.[10]

We spoke in the introduction of an attentive intentionality required of a singular vessel of devotion gathered in unity to invoke the living God, to sing God's praises in one voice, and to empty themselves in self-offering in union with Christ as a gift returned for a gift received. This is, as Chauvet says, a "mystery of faith," whose priority over the eucharistic species and the priest who "confects" sounds blasphemous to many pious believers. But once again, we assert that unless we gather as a sacramental Body to pray and acknowledge our need, to hear the word as a constituent part of our own story as a people and to be convicted by it, and then to join in the great procession to open our hands to receive the food and drink that seals that covenant...unless we "do this in memory of Him," *per ipsum, et cum ipso, et in ipso*, there can be no Eucharist, no blessed sacrament, and no holy communion. Chauvet goes so far as to call this recognition the "primary scandal" of God's saving acts in Jesus. Even more, *not to recognize this sacramental mystery* in the "concrete assembly" is a harsh reality that confronts us each time we gather to be the faithful remnant of those clothed in Christ in baptism and intimately "woven in one piece from the top" (John 19:23) *in ipso*, and who now devote themselves "to the breaking of bread and the prayers," as the author of Acts called the early gatherings (Acts 2:42). Honoring that identity and letting the liturgy express it by taking the movements, gestures, and choreography of the assembly's role in the liturgy seriously is the response to this challenge and confronts the "already" but very much more the "not yet" of our vocation to be this singular vessel we were and are being formed to be. Participation, from this perspective, is not merely a notional assent to what the presider says and does. It is full-bodied, transparent, and challenging—and often not very efficient! Trusting this involves a deep call to faith.

Twentieth-century Orthodox sacramental theologian Alexander Schmemann impresses upon us in so many ways the radical reimagination that must take place if we are to celebrate the sacred mysteries faithfully as a sacramental Body. In one particularly poignant passage from his seminal book *For the Life of the World: Sacraments and Orthodoxy*, Schmemann says,

The journey begins when Christians leave their homes and beds. They leave, indeed, their life in this present and concrete world, and whether they have to drive fifteen miles or walk a few blocks, a sacramental act is already taking place, *an act that is the very condition of everything else that is to happen*. For they are now on their way to *constitute the Church*, or to be more exact, to be transformed into the Church of God. They have been individuals…the "natural" world and a natural community. And now they have been called to "come together in one place," to bring their lives, their very "world" with them and to be more than what they were: a *new* community with a new life.[11]

Everything in the journey speaks to how the body manifests the Body.

THE GESTURES OF WELCOME IMPRINTED ON THE BODY

The newness of which Schmemann speaks is not simply a figure of an interior cohesion. It is rooted in "their lives, their very 'world,'" which is the embodied context of the ordinary gathering of individual believers now emptying themselves out in order to be filled with a new identity together in Christ, a "true Body and a Mystical Body." Once again, a specific and readily available example may help to deepen the discussion. When the Church celebrates the welcoming of new candidates and catechumens for reception into the Catholic faith, she receives them at the door into the Sunday assembly and then signs their bodies in a tactile, expressive gesture of imprinting the attitudes of this sacramental Body into their own journey toward full communion with the Catholic Church. "Receive the sign of the cross on your hands, shoulders, mouth, forehead, feet, and heart," the prayer says in words that are accompanied by a very embodied act of blessing. Hands to receive, shoulders to bear the yoke, a mouth to give testimony to what God is doing in our midst, feet to walk the journey, a heart whose inside matches this exterior proclamation taking place in each of these seeking souls…the ministers impress on these bodies in the form of a cross the attitudes and life of this Body before whom they stand, a

34

Body who sees in these candidates and catechumens its own single-hearted vocation to deepen in this "mystery of faith" of which Chauvet marvels.

Why does the presider not simply read a script and it is done? Why is it necessary that he, along with other ministers of formation or leaders of the community, approach these individuals with both word and gesture, in the witness of this assembly, and trace the very sign upon all these parts of their bodies, which together represent their wholeness as unique persons created in God's image? The gesture is "significant" and bears a reality that begins an initiation into this singular vessel of devotion she manifests. It is true and it is mystical; it happens *here* in this place, with *these people*, in the presence of *this community* as a bearer of a reality that a simple proclamation or fiat can never express adequately. Christ has called them to "come and see," and they have responded by their inquiry and decision to join the formation community by coming forward—which itself is a great "mystery of faith" on their own parts—and asking again of the Church, Christ's Body, "Where are you staying?" and "Where do you live?" The Body responds to their self-offering by imprinting on these bodies the mystical truth of this sacramental Body in a gesture of welcome. "*Here* is where we are. *This* is who we are." As the *Catechism of the Catholic Church* says about moments of celebrations such as this, "In the age of the Church, between the Passover of Christ already accomplished once for all, and its consummation in the kingdom of God, the liturgy celebrated...bears the imprint of the newness of the mystery of Christ" (1164).

Something new is being born in these candidates and catechumens, which also means that something is being refashioned in the Body of Christ herself. Everything in this rich interchange *forms*. Given such an assertion, it remains difficult to explain with a linear logic what is going on in this rite of welcome and acceptance, nor is it efficient to take the time the rite asks to trace carefully this cross that spans the heights and depths of all desire, but when a community celebrates this in fullness of sign and symbol and gesture and movement, the meaning is disclosed. It is a revelatory moment whose privileged vehicle is this singular vessel and her ritual actions celebrated with attentive intentionality. This is true of all corporate public liturgy. Its nature is relational, dialogical, and participative, as we said earlier, and liturgical prayer needs a body to enable the Body to be a sacramental communion; even more, it needs *these* bodies in her Body because "the love of Christ urges [her] on" (2 Cor 5:14), and the pierced heart of the Father seeks these inquirers and lures them with a love beyond all imagining. The dynamism at the center of the liturgy is the hallowing of the Holy Spirit, not simply as a grace from the top down, but a graceful movement flowing through and with and in Christ animated by love, a love now face-to-face in this liturgical moment with these new pilgrims. Hence, the importance of the signing of their bodies signifies this grace with a clarity that risks being lost when the gestures and dynamics of personal encounter are minimalized.

What do these movements and gestures teach? First, they announce that the worshiping assembly is always the learning one, clinging to Christ, because the seekers who come stir their own seeking. But, at the same time, because Christ clings to her, the sacramental Body is also the teacher who invites and shares the reality of these saving mysteries. She imparts this mystical truth not simply by *being* the Body of Christ, but by enacting and celebrating it as "communion incarnate." "*This* is my Body." To echo Fagerberg again, "Mystery is not something to know, it is something to be and do."[12]

Countless theologians and spiritual writers from patristic times to the present have tried to capture the "intentional ambiguity" that the paradox of a lived and celebrated practice of the faith in a broken world and Church entails. For example, St. Augustine's homilies to the newly baptized in the fourth century are perhaps the most poignant and often-cited reference to the concrete corporeality of the sacramental Body as the locus and site of the presence and action of Christ's saving mysteries in our midst. He exclaims in a powerful preaching moment,

> Believers show they know the Body of Christ if they do not neglect to be the Body of Christ. Let them become the Body of Christ....It is for this that the Apostle Paul, expounding on this bread, says: "Because the loaf of bread is one, we, many though we are, are one body" (1 Cor 10:17). O sacrament of devotion! O sign of unity! O bond of charity! He that would live has where to live, has whence to live. Let him draw near, let him believe; let him become part of the Body, that he may be made to live....Thus, the Lord would have this food and drink to be understood as meaning the fellowship of his own Body and members, which is the holy Church.[13]

36

In the mid-twentieth century, Henri de Lubac discovered this in numerous early texts that bear great meaning for any contemporary assembly today. For example, when speaking of the "paradoxical significance" where Eucharist and the Church are respectively named *true body* and *mystical body*, he quotes Arnold of Bonneval, twelfth-century Cistercian abbot and confrere of Bernard of Clairvaux:

> Just as in the person of Christ the humanity was seen and the divinity was hidden; so the divine essence poured itself ineffably into the visible sacrament, so that religion should include devotion round the sacraments, and also that there be a more full access to the truth whose body and blood the sacraments are.[14]

Contemporary writers like Benedictine Ghislain Lafont note the assembly's ritual locus as the clarifying moment of a cosmic act of redemption. Attempting to plumb the *mysterium fidei* we proclaim and into which we are consecrated and transformed, he begins by asserting the primacy of the liturgical encounter as the teacher par excellence of the "event remembered" in Christ's saving deeds, insisting

> that no historical or theoretical reflection on the death and resurrection of Jesus Christ can attain to the fullness of reality and significance that these events take on when they are remembered in the Eucharistic liturgy....The truth of the story is not independent of the person to whom it addressed or of the situation of the one telling it.[15]

He then goes on to sharpen the contours of that rhythm and harmony of the liturgy as the place where that sacramental Body can articulate such an "ineffable Mystery." He says,

> Thus, the place where the paschal mystery is recounted with the greatest truth and the most realism is not a theology book or in catechetical instruction. These come before or after, but they only have value when joined to the living invocation of God, which is never full as it is in the Eucharist. The true history is a poem of thanksgiving.[16]

Note that Lafont speaks of the "fullness of reality" and the "significance" of these mysteries. The "place" of its revelation yields "the greatest truth and the most realism." And the vehicle is the liturgy of the vessel that holds and embodies this treasure. Fittingly, he calls this "a poem of thanksgiving." To begin to imagine the movements of the Body as part of a poetic enactment releases us from the slavery of rubrics as the first and only arbiters of truth and what is *justo y necesario*, as the Spanish text testifies to the truth of this gathering to give praise and thanks.[17] Rubrical efficiency and precision pale before the rhythm and harmony and cadence of ritual poetry. A closer look at the dynamism of poetic acts will make the rest of the discussion of gesture and choreography rich and evocative.

THE POETRY OF "THE SKIN'S MEMORY" IN EVERYDAY WORSHIP

The liturgical poem, like all poetry, is always attentive to the arrangements of each element in precisely a certain way and order such that a rhythm develops when the elements of matter and form *act together* to embody something richer than the words alone. They communicate a "whole" where movement, gesture, evocative word,[18] and the assembly's interior disposition conspire together to realize the prayer of the Church. Lafont speaks of the distinctive characteristics and "founding discourse" of the poem we call corporal public worship. He says, "Its language is unique, at once human and surpassing what is human…a song addressed to God, a response to the name that God has given, a passing beyond merely human limits."[19] The character of this poem is dialogical, relational, and participative, to use terminology we employed for the rhythm of the liturgical pattern. Embodied persons with histories of faith are *justo y necesario* in this song of praise. As he says,

> In its turn, the word reveals the human being. It immediately shows the human being to be a being of communion. There are no words except *words exchanged*. And the word defines the symbolic field of communion: music. Each one of us is a voice for others—a song and a melody.[20]

Gifts given and received and offered back are all put to material work by the sacramental Body gathered in this liturgical poetics, producing what we call "holy communion" and "consecration" and what Lafont considers unitive in all this, *transfiguration.*[21] In this transfigured reality, God's desire is placed next to a people's seeking, and at the center of this relationship is the invitation to gather through, with, and in the person of Christ, Word made flesh, who is "true God and true man." The Holy Spirit expresses that bond of unity between Father and Son, now overflowing in and through this Body in the poetry of the rite. The singular vessel of devotion gathered in this place stands before the living God and sings her *fiat*, in response to all prayer and action evoked in this poem: "Amen. So be it." That is why matter *matters* and form *forms*. The liturgical poem is not the poem unless the relationality and cadence are given full expression in the liturgical enactment.

Another contemporary liturgical theologian, Nathan Mitchell, also wrestled with liturgical poetics in order to reveal a mystery hidden in the ordinary, or, as he quotes Latino systematic theologian Orlando Espín, "within the context of *lo cotidiano*," what is most ordinary in matter and form. The poetic interplay of rhythm and harmony and emptiness is "the vital connection between thought (cognition) and embodied ritual (practice)." Something new emerges that is, to use the terms we have been employing, "true and mystical," sacred and yet "fruit of the earth and work of human hands," as the preparation rite proclaims. More importantly to the specificity of the assembly praying, Mitchell locates the site of that new reality as embedded in the body celebrating. He says, regarding this practice in Hispanic literature and religious practice, which employs such poetry in rich profusion, "This poetics of religious (re)creation is not merely—or primarily—cognitive; it is born of the body, inscribed on the body. It constitutes a veritable *poetics of the body*."[22] That is why, in another reflection on the poetics of space, to which we will return later in the book, he highlights the important role of "the skin's memory, the body's wisdom, and the geometry of prayer" in every communal act of worship.[23]

All of this suggests that how the body assembles, the gestures she uses, and how this interrelationship is reverenced and set out clearly between the actors and the elements in this "poetics of space" are participants in the beauty and truth being expressed in the act of praying. To use the example of the signing of the senses in the welcoming rite for candidates and catechumens: these bodies placed in the midst of the sacramental Body, the touch of the leader (and others) of that Body who gather the community into communion as Christ's Body, along with the imprinting of the sign of the cross are all necessary for the cadence and harmony of this poetics of worship. Layer upon layer in this matrix of symbolic relationships generate the circulation of grace that both gathers in the assembly to draw her into communion with Christ and one another, as then opens her hands and heart to create a space for these new ones, signs and symbols themselves of our ever-deepening pilgrimage to our true home. Such generativity that employs the sacramental vehicle of matter and form asks, within the rhythm of the whole interior attitude of Christ's mind and heart, that such actions and gestures and context be taken seriously. As the venerable Yves Congar once asserted regarding lackluster preaching, we can also argue that liturgical rites, when they become *pro forma* and perfunctory, may not even attain the *res tantum* of the sacrament, that is, the grace of union with Christ in the soul.[24] And the "soul" here, as we have said, is the assembly's soul and deepest center, where she clings to Christ and Christ clings to her.

THE SIGN OF THE CROSS ON BODIES AND HOLY THINGS AS SIGN AND SYMBOL OF THE COVENANTAL BOND OF THE SACRAMENTAL BODY

The importance of commonplace gestures such as tracing a cross are not *pro forma* or inconsequential, although many times the action is unconscious, such as when entering a Church or honoring the tabernacle with a genuflection. The first formal gesture of the gathered community when the presider enters the sanctuary is this communal sign of the cross, traced on all the participants' bodies and giving a cruciform shape to the name in which they gather. The depth of meaning intensifies when employed throughout the liturgy, especially when it is a recognized liturgical gesture and act, such as signing the Gospel book before its proclamation, accompanied by a communal sign of the cross inscribed on the forehead, the lips, and the heart of the proclaimer in union with the assembly's response. The presider's blessing with the sign for the deacon who will proclaim the Gospel in the name of the gathered Church is really a prayerful expression of this outward sign of an interior grace that will be traced upon his body and those of the sacramental Body present. What is more, his prayer is really a moment of the whole assembly's being summoned to receive the message and grace of this revelatory word by means of bodily acts and in the name of the triune communion. The accompanying movement of all standing to honor that life-giving word passed on "in their hearing" at this moment of proclamation testifies its truth precisely through the deacon's role as the voice and herald of this Gospel, addressed to the *ekklesia* in its sacramental bond of unity. The prayer of the presider says,

> May the Lord be in your heart and on your lips,
> That you may proclaim his Gospel worthily and well,
> In the name of the Father and of the Son, and of the Holy
> Spirit.[25]

The action the prayer invokes begs that the Lord inscribe that christic identity into every fabric of our "communion incarnate" so that we may worthily proclaim and hear the revelatory message contained in the textual words. This is not simply a cognitive knowing, but a *sentir*, a felt knowledge whose truth and mystery unfolds within the multivalent action itself. In standing together, all turned toward the ambo and the Gospel book, and in the signing of their bodies in a mutual expression of oneness in Christ, the Body proclaims that she is ready and willing to hear the word and be convicted by it. It is a fitting gesture, on behalf of the sacramental Body, that the deacon, priest, or bishop then kisses the Gospel book. The "holy kiss" is one of the tradition's most evocative signs of intimacy and communion.[26]

So it can be said without exaggeration that this embodied reception of a proclaimed and preached word[27] into the holy house and in the hearing of this singular vessel of devotion is the necessary fiat for any further movement toward the communion of the liturgy. The nourishment of hearing the word and receiving it in this formal fashion—sealed with the sign of the cross—stirs the hunger and thirst that leads to joining in Christ's own self-offering at the table of Eucharist. What

41

the Body enacts here at the ambo makes Eucharist possible, for the community is born out of the Word made flesh. Indeed, Christ is present *here*, "when the holy scriptures are read in the Church," really and truly (SC 7). It begins the saving narrative, of which the whole sacramental event is, as Karl Rahner says, "a single work" bestowing grace.[28] We will investigate the wholeness of Word and Sacrament within the liturgy in the following chapter, exploring the bodily dimensions of their intrinsic unity, which the Constitution on the Sacred Liturgy maintains as being "so closely connected with each other that they form a single act of worship" (SC 56). Gathering to sign their bodies as one Body within the liturgy effects what it signifies, for what is true in the liturgy as a whole is mirrored in the assembly "in the Name of the Father, and of the Son, and of the Holy Spirit." The gathered Church, the Body of Christ, now takes its shape within what Augustine and later Church documents refer to as an integral bond of identity, in both "the table of the Word" and "the table of the Eucharist."[29] All sacramental celebrations of this twofold event of the Body at prayer are, as Pope Benedict XVI described them, "encounters with the Risen Lord."[30] The communal sign of the cross is simply an expression of this triune unity that spirals toward the altar and holy communion.

THE SIGN OF THE CROSS AS AN INITIATORY SYMBOL OF IDENTITY WITH THE *TOTUS CHRISTUS*

We can ponder the beauty of the cycle and rhythm here: the signing of the body in the rite of welcome for new members of this universal Body is reenacted at every liturgy and within every liturgical assembly. In a very real sense, in our own ritual signing, we are the nurslings again, soon to be born; and those who are initially welcomed by our signing of them represent us, fellow pilgrims who gather to "constitute the Church," as Schmemann said. This is the ambiguous intentionality of liturgical poetics! The tent is wide and always has "plenty good room,"[31] the traditional African American spiritual sings it, for all to "come mingle" with this richly diverse, multicultural, and intergenerational horde, all born from the womb of the fecund Mother, and we sisters and brothers are in communion with those who have gone before us and those still to come. As the fifth-century baptistery inscription at the Lateran Basilica in Rome vividly describes,

> The brood born here to live in heaven has life
> from water and the fructifying Spirit....
> The stream that flows below sprang
> from the wounded Christ.

The sign of the cross, therefore, reaching with the expansive arms of Christ embracing the world, descending to the depths of all reality and ascending to the heights, has been passed into us, lives now, and will be our enduring truth. The reality we embody by this memorial and eschatological action locates in time and space this Body as a singular vessel of this devotion, born from the same maternal font. It incorporates the nature of devotion itself, a "profound dedication by means of solemn and formal act," as we defined earlier. Needless to say, such profound gestures should be intentional and significant, and the ambiguous identity of Christ as Head of the members of his Body who hungers and thirsts should be intensified in our doing it, and it speaks within that act the longing of all creation for redemption. These layers of meaning expressed in action are part of the poetics of liturgical expression. And they are based "within the context of *lo cotidiano*," what is most ordinary in matter and form. Gathered as one in the triune name, "*This* is my Body."

Once an assembly begins to be intentionally attentive and in rhythm in common with both the inside and outside of these liturgical rites, so much richness begins to emerge. A simple gesture such as bathing the hands in the font when entering the church building or bowing the head to feel the waters of the *asperges* carries "the skin's memory, the body's wisdom, and the geometry of prayer," to remember Mitchell's imagery. When done in tandem with the grace flowing from the inside to the outside, the hand descending, the water marking the body on forehead, breast, and shoulders, and then our entering into the threshold of the holy house...all this communicates a "communion incarnate" that is imprinted soul-fully and gracefully through attentive practice. This is the hope of attentive intentionality of such simple movements: individuals hand themselves over in this gesture and identify with the Body who worships here, which is inseparable from the

Christ who is Head and heart for these limbs and the vine that engrafts these branches, so that "it is no longer I who live, but it is Christ who lives in me" (Gal 2:20). This is a living grace, Paul says further, and not a law or litmus test of membership (v. 21). Imagining through this intentional act the true Body and the mystical Body and our one Body, we may be tempted to ask, "How can this be?" Like Mary, *Mater ecclesiae*, this is the beginning of our handing over in a focal way the birth of awe and wonder, the proper attitude of a eucharistic people. It gives credence to Tertullian's famous axiom: *Caro salutis est cardo* (The flesh is the hinge of salvation).[32] Without the hinge, there is no door; without the door of welcome and identity, the temple is empty of her purpose and sacredness. All this is happening when signing the body with the sign of the cross and mixing that act with the richness of initiation and fonts and a gathered assembly that shares this gesture as an identifying mark of the sacramental Body. The simplest and most repetitive gestures can truly matter and form.

ANOINTING AS THE BALM AND THE WHOLENESS OF SACRAMENTAL SOUL AND BODY

The same communal bond takes place with the ritual act of anointing—the fragrant, sensual balm that communicates healing, hallowing, and mission. The effusive character of this matter and form makes great claims upon those who anoint and those who hand themselves over to be anointed. It provides another compelling example of how liturgical gesture and action consecrate the Body and allow the rhythm and harmony of the rite to be expressed.

Fundamental in this consideration is the centrality of Christ, who is himself "the Anointed One," whom Peter announces as the long sought-for Messiah (John 1:41). He is the chosen one, in the line of David and Solomon and the leaders of the people that God chooses and protects.[33] The people, in his name, inherit the blessing such leadership for mission imparts. He shares the mission of the prophet Habakkuk, who prays to the Lord in the name of all to whom he is sent: "You came forth to save your people, to save your anointed" (Hab 3:13). To be chosen and gathered and given a name means that the people share the anointing of the Holy One. This gesture, then, takes on christological significance for the Christian community who remains faithful, those whom 1 John 2:20 calls "you [who] have been anointed by the Holy One, and all of you [who] have knowledge." The liturgical gesture of anointing manifests the sign of the indwelling Spirit that makes whole and gives discernment and direction to the Body. The "oil of gladness" (Isa 61:3; Heb 1:9) shared in the rite is the community's insignia that makes explicit the interior reality of willingness and receptivity that this unifying grace imparts as the Body clings to Christ and Christ to them. In his advent, Christ's own grace of "communion incarnate" with the Father is now, in the ritual act, the Body's own communion in him. In this sense, as Paul says,

> For in him every one of God's promises is a "Yes." For this reason it is through him that we say the "Amen," to the glory of God. But it is God who establishes us with you in Christ and has anointed us, by putting his seal on us and giving us his Spirit in our hearts as a first installment. (2 Cor 1:20–22)

When that wholeness is somehow sundered or weakened through the vicissitudes of life, the anointing within the assembly restores, heals, comforts, and announces the promise that the Body of Christ will not desert the sister or brother. Indeed, the ritual act is not for the individual alone, but is a rite that seeks restoration from the fragmentation that sinfulness, illness, or despair wrecks upon the whole Body. In the scriptural word that accompanies the rite of anointing of the sick, the writer of James instructs the community to "call for the elders of the church and have them pray over them, anointing them with oil in the name of the Lord" (Jas 5:14).

Anointing, then, whether it be for commission (in confirmation and orders) or strength and healing (in the anointing of the sick), is always a raising up into the arms of the *totus Christus*, an ecclesial embrace poured out upon individuals. The ritual gesture, precisely as a sacramental action, is sign and symbol of the wholeness for which the entire Body longs and cannot rest until she rests in that communion of Father, Son, and Holy Spirit. Personal healing, commission, and ordination, therefore, always point to the unity of the Body of Christ;

45

every anointing is communal. As St. Paul reminds the Corinthian community, "Indeed, the body does not consist of one member but of many…[and] the members of the body that seem to be weaker are indispensable," and "if one member suffers, all suffer together with it; if one member is honored, all rejoice together with it" (1 Cor 12:14, 22, 26). This membership in the one Body, Paul goes on to recount, has incumbent upon her the mind and heart of Christ, each a balm expressed for the whole in the individuality of gift and need. It is after this exhortation that the seminal discourse upon the primacy of love in 1 Corinthians 13 is set forward and makes profound sense from the perspective of anointing. "And now faith, hope, and love abide, these three; and the greatest of these is love" (v. 13).

What binds this common gesture of anointing—whether for initiation, exorcism, confirmation, ordination, or healing—is that all carry within them this intensification of the love and presence of Christ and "communion incarnate" in the sacramental Body. Every time the community gathers to "do this in memory of Him," the interior attitude rises up from the fontal depths in thanks and praise and expresses itself in such a sensual medium as "communion incarnate." This image is so persistent in St. Paul's letters to the communities. He exhorts the Corinthian community to reconciliation and wholeness, in light of his experience of believers in Troas and Macedonia in particular, by giving voice to the liturgical character of the grace of chrismation as a poetic description of the community itself. He says,

> But thanks be to God, who in Christ always leads us in triumphal procession, and through us spreads in every place the fragrance that comes from knowing him. For we are the aroma of Christ…persons sent from God and standing in his presence. (2 Cor 2:14–15a, 17b)

The richness of this gesture in the midst of a community, therefore, spans the heights of gladness and joy, the rich depths of being chosen and missioned in the power of the Spirit, and reaches into every soul in the Body's soul in the times of greatest fragility and alienation. Even evil spirits are exorcized through this action, and so the ritual gesture announces that no one and nothing can remain victorious over those who are bound to Christ, the Father's Anointed One, in the power of the Spirit. Given the central role this plays in Head and members, in their baptismal identity and confirming mission, in the commission of her ministers and the care of her weak ones, it seems that the gesture of anointing deserves such intentional attention and fullness of expression. As the rite for the blessing of oils and the consecration of chrism expresses,

> Therefore we beseech you, Lord:
> be pleased to sanctify with your + blessing this oil in its richness,
> and to pour into it the strength of the Holy Spirit,
> with the powerful working of your Christ.
> From his holy name it has received the name of Chrism,
> and with it you have anointed your priests, prophets, kings, and
>   martyrs.
>
> May you confirm the Chrism you have created
> as a sacred sign of perfect salvation and life
> for those to be made new in the spiritual waters of Baptism.
>
> May those formed into a temple of your majesty
> by the holiness infused through this anointing
> and by the cleansing of the stain of their first birth
> be made fragrant with the innocence of a life pleasing to you.[34]

This blessing has its own epiclesis, just as the Eucharistic Prayer invokes the hallowing of the Spirit, as the bishop, in the name of the Church, stretches out his hands, imploring the Father of all good gifts that "by the power of your love, make this mixture of oil and perfume a sign and a source of your blessing." In this outpouring of gifts, it continues, "Let the splendor of holiness shine on the world from every place and thing signed with this oil." Clearly, the prayers of the rite announce what the very physical gesture and movement enacts. The best of who we are as a priestly people, whose seed and root are the apostles and martyrs, is lavished upon all—saint and sinner—so that the holy dwelling and singular vessel of devotion may be sanctified, radiant, christic, forgiven, and made whole. The Eastern Catholic theologian Jean Corbon calls this an expression of "the sacramental harmony of the Body of Christ."[35] There is a broad reach in God's touch expressed here, which testifies to the wideness of the tent, the depth of mercy, the closeness of Christ, the primal source in God the Creator of all the heavens and earth, made present in and consecrating "every place and thing signed

47

by this oil." Truly, the sign signifies a reality that is a rich matrix of symbolic relationships and "bears the imprint of the newness of the mystery of Christ" (CCC 1164).

With the attentive intentionality such a grace demands, the gestures and movements we use to signify such a treasure should be mined for all the treasure such matter and form entail. Anointing in the name of the Lord highlights the important role of "the skin's memory, the body's wisdom, and the geometry of prayer," in this highly expressive poetics the rite invites us to embrace. A closer look at its communal movements and gestures, therefore, deserves attention.

Liturgical theologian Antonio Donghi, in speaking of the specifically physical characteristics of the action, reinforces the importance of both matter and form in this action:

> The gesture of anointing possesses a particular symbolic meaning. The oil passes from the skin into the body. The heat thus generated places the muscles in optimal condition to follow the commands of the will. The oil warms the muscles, making them malleable and agile, as in the experience of athletes.[36]

Given this rich depth of the body as vehicle of an interior/exterior harmony, it seems important to note that for the sacramental *sign* to move into the order of *symbol*, it must be embodied in such a way that it invites the individual into the whole. Louis-Marie Chauvet insists that this reaching out and drawing one into the wholeness, "an order of which it is itself a part," is essential to any symbol's function, for the matter and form "crystallizes into itself the whole," all so that it may be "recognized" and by that recognition "unifying," so that the one experiencing the symbol is "bonded together" in a "common symbolic order and allows them to form a *community*." In short, "The symbol is a mediator of identity only by being a *creator of community*."[37] Given the sacramental economy in which anointing plays such a strategic role, its meaning as a creative and effusive agent of bonding with the Body is most vital when its liturgical enactment is expressive and transparent.

In light of the emphasis above on the individual action as a sign and symbol of the whole, we could say that the three holy oils used in baptizing, confirming, ordaining, and healing are exercising and preparing the entire Body to act with vigor and malleability, all in response to the Spirit's hallowing and in union with her Head, whose aroma is sweet and fragrant, signaling a holy presence particularly and sensually, and yet never simply confined to this person or this place. The balm needs human hands to massage its healing effects upon another body, so that the whole Body comes to know and experience the divine touch that is always and everywhere being offered. And the divine touch cannot reach the fullness of its *res tantum* in this ritual act unless "communion incarnate" is genuinely experienced as the site and locus of its saving effects.

The fullness of the sign challenges the celebration of liturgical rites to allow the affective restoration to the whole the symbol promises to become a reality. Baptismal anointing, as rich and full as possible, surrounded by a family and community around the font, communicates the efficacy of the true and mystical Body and allows the deep meaning of the initiation rite to be unambiguously transparent. Those who receive chrismation in the rites of initiation and confirmation might discover the ecclesial and communal effects of this sacred action with greater transparency when the gesture is carried out in the aisles, with enough oil and tender massaging to be able to carry the weight of this symbolic matter and form, surrounded by the touch of the community and ministers. The areas of the body are important in all anointing rites, such as the head and breast and the hands, the nostrils and the ears, as in some early fifth-century Roman liturgies, and even "in the place where the illness is most acute," as an eighth-century sacramentary prescribes. The sacramental matter and form in these anointings demonstrate a profound commingling of the physical body of these individuals who are baptized, confirmed, ordained for ministry, or in need of the reconciliation and healing Christ offers. In these ecclesial actions, they are truly united with the *Corpus Christi* celebrating in their midst. Anointing in the power of the Holy Spirit then can be seen as a balm for the whole Body, and the Church as acting in communion with the Anointed One, as both giver and receiver of the gift.[38] Intentionality and an awareness of the "outward sign of an inward reality" call the praying Church to take these gestures and movements and choreography seriously. Settling as we often do for a largely inconsequential smudge from a presider, largely observed from afar by the very community whose "geometry of prayer" constructs the holy house and singular vessel of devotion, mutes the proclamation the matter and form convey, rather than expressing and testifying to the symbolic

49

exchange in the movement of grace from the skin of one individual into "the skin's memory" of the sacramental Body.

Oil taken from a cotton swab, mechanically and sparingly applied, provides a paltry sign that risks edging itself out of the symbolic order. Attentive intentionality is not liturgical fussiness or overdramatization, a critique often leveled to hide our fear of the sensual power of matter and form to communicate the absolute seriousness of the divine passion at the source of Christ's gathering and the Spirit's hallowing. Inside and outside coinhere through oil, touch, and comforting word of faith in this Body.

Simple conclusions follow that flow from the many aspects of this particular expression of the "geometry of prayer." Anointing, as we said, always raises up and makes new. The intentionality and expressiveness for both the oil and the movement of anointing and the presence of the community in the midst of these anointed ones affirms and intensifies a new identity in a "geometry of prayer" of ritual action, which Mitchell called the appropriate vehicle for "the skin's memory" and "the body's wisdom," all encased in a "veritable *poetics of the body*."[39] Chrismation is the insignia of this hallowing. Done with exuberance that is also restrained and dignified, an intentional ambiguity in itself that demands an artfulness and a choreography, liturgical anointing is a solemn endeavor and also a very tender inscribing of "communion incarnate," whose pleasant and charismatic fragrance should linger long after the rite has ended and the community dispersed. It announces that the Shepherd to whom we cling and who clings to this Body truly "restores (our) soul," as the Psalmist says, and makes the liturgical celebration of word and table find its sacramental fulfillment[40] as a communal revelation and a shared meal, a word that testifies and food that is pure gift from above:

> You prepare a table before me
>   in the presence of my enemies;
> you anoint my head with oil;
>   my cup overflows.
> Surely goodness and mercy shall follow me
>   all the days of my life,
> and I shall dwell in the house of the LORD
>   my whole life long. (Ps 23:5–6)

There is no linear logic or efficiency in giving the gesture of anointing its due symbolic significance. But when the sacramental Body allows it full sway, the meaning inheres.

> Thanks be to God, who in Christ always leads us in triumphal procession, and through us spreads in every place the fragrance that comes from knowing him. For we are the aroma of Christ...persons sent from God and standing in his presence. (2 Cor 2:14–15a, 17b)

COMMUNAL STANDING, KNEELING, AND PROCESSING AS BODILY DEVOTION

Liturgical posture, in these very ordinary and abundant movements within the liturgy, is the sacramental Body's primal choreography, and not simply the permitted directives by the appointed minister. Their transparency and dynamism as "matter" and "form" become much clearer when they express an interior unity rather than a personal pious preference. Here we can say that uniformity of movement and its patterned and graceful embodiment play a special role in increasing the devotion of the singular vessel at prayer. Granted, each gesture and movement here has a level of meaning for an individual person, but when the common dance of gesture begins to act within a sacramental Body, a deeper sacramental bonding and "communion incarnate" is bodied forth as a radiant sign and symbol of the *Corpus Christi* at prayer. There is a freedom in a worshiping assembly that is unveiled in conformity to a liturgical cadence, whose pattern, over time, inscribes that communion from the inside to the outside. It is "spiritual choreography" in the best sense of that term. As Paul says,

> Now the Lord is the Spirit, and where the Spirit of the Lord is, there is freedom. And all of us, with unveiled faces, seeing the glory of the Lord as though reflected in a mirror, are being transformed into the same image from one degree of

glory to another; for this comes from the Lord, the Spirit. (2 Cor 3:17–18)

The matter and form of these liturgical movements within the context of *lo cotidiano* manifest a charism and a gift poured out upon those whom the Spirit draws into union with Christ to offer praise and thanks to the Father in "a willing and holy surrender of themselves."[41] From a meditative theology approach to the liturgy we celebrate, we can attest that if we were not convoked to enact this kenotic movement, the transformation of these ordinary actions would not be "unveiled" and we could not dance together with such beauty. The individual steps back and a new Body begins to move as one. A closer look at these three gestures and movements can illuminate the unifying grace at work in liturgical posture.

The 2010 General Instruction of the Roman Missal speaks of the transparency of communal bodily actions. In a section of chapter 2, entitled "Gestures and Bodily Posture," it says,

> The gestures and bodily posture of both the Priest, the Deacon, and the ministers, and also of the people, must be conducive to making the entire celebration resplendent with beauty and noble simplicity, to making clear the true and full meaning of its different parts, and to fostering the participation of all. Attention must therefore be paid to what is determined by this General Instruction and by the traditional practice of the Roman Rite and to what serves the common spiritual good of the People of God, rather than private inclination or arbitrary choice.
>
> A common bodily posture, to be observed by all those taking part, is a sign of the unity of the members of the Christian community gathered together for the Sacred Liturgy, for it expresses the intentions and spiritual attitude of the participants and also fosters them.[42]

The purpose of the uniformity of gestures such as standing, kneeling, and processing galvanizes the assembly in this "poem of thanksgiving" so that a unified choreography throughout the entire celebration radiates beauty in noble simplicity, while contributing to the "full and true meaning" of the poetics situated within the matrix of symbolic relationships. As an outward expression of an interior unity, the intentional and attentive *participation of all* "is demanded by the very nature of the liturgy," as SC 14 insists. Head and members together are called to *do* something in order to *be* someone together, "(and) is their right and duty by reason of their baptism," as the Vatican document emphasized. Acting in rhythm and harmony as a constitutive act of their very identity as the Body of Christ is not simply preferable, the document goes on to say, but "this full and active participation by all the people is the aim to be considered before all else, for it is the primary source from which the faithful are to derive the true Christian spirit" (SC 14). Entrance into the spirit and movement of the liturgy in this spirit of the *totus Christus* forms a sacramental Body "with devotion and full involvement" (no. 48). The necessity of personal and intentional engagement is crucial and central to clinging to Christ and we to him. Liturgical participation is "demanded" not because it is imposed from some disembodied rubric from above, from those who possess a sacred treasure and are giving it to those under their care; rather, the nature of a baptized people cannot but act in this unified expression of praise and thanks. Romano Guardini called this nature and principle a movement of the Spirit and a summons to a vibrant communion by the Head for the members, an action of "Christ Himself; His life is ours; we are incorporated in Him; we are His Body, *Corpus mysticum*. The active force which governs this living unity, grafting the individual on to it, granting [the person] a share in its fellowship and preserving this right for him, is the Holy Ghost."[43] The sacramental Body, therefore, by exercising her identity, cannot be accused of willfulness or some misplaced focus on her importance here. Like all actions of this Body, acting together enacts a handing over to the *totus Christus*, from willfulness to willingness. The agent and bond of this communion, Guardini says, is the Holy Spirit, and where the Spirit is, grace is flowing around and through and within each faithful one, in a creative act of refashioning of a Body that is, to echo Paul again, "being transformed into the same image from one degree of glory to another; for this comes from the Lord, the Spirit" (2 Cor 3:18). Participation, therefore, is not something we first elect to do, but the Spirit-filled manifestation of the *ekklesia*, those convoked to express the triune life inscribed into them.

Consistent with the inside-to-outside attitude we have been exploring, standing or kneeling is not, as especially happens when communities are fractured and at odds, an expression of one's "private inclination or arbitrary choice." Surely and commendably, each of these gestures and movements has a rich meaning when done by individuals alone. But when expressed together in the sacred dance of praise and thanks, a deeper revelation of unity in Christ and one another takes place in a privileged way that makes individual gestures of piety *always* secondary. And when the practice of these repetitive gestures faithfully celebrated over time enters "the skin's memory" and the "body's wisdom," the "geometry of prayer" is liberating and communicates to the Body a new sense of its identity and communion, what GIRM 42 called "the sign of unity" of the gathered Body, which "expresses the intentions and spiritual attitude of the participants and also fosters them." Affective union deepens, then, with practice. Standing, kneeling, and processing, we will now see, each possess the capacity to intensify that sacramental bond of "one body, one Spirit in Christ."

Standing together in the holy house is perhaps the most ordinary and most often overlooked posture to consider in light of the spiritual attitude it bodies forth. In his short and accessible book entitled *Sacred Signs*, Romano Guardini roots the interior attitude of this ordinary act in terms of the dignity of those who stand and the reverence due to God, before whom they stand as a community in praise and thanks. He says, quite simply, "The respect we owe to the infinite God requires of us a bearing suited to such a presence." The upright posture suggests the sacramental Body is claiming her identity as the Body of Christ, for "to stand up means that we are in possession of ourselves...we stand, as it were, at attention, geared and ready for action."[44] Attentive intentionality deepens that possession, for standing together, then, is not simply a bodily position but a bonding expression that we are *now* in this mystery together. A few practical examples may help here, namely from the penitential rite and the Eucharistic Prayer.

The opening rites of the liturgy are often weighed down by numerous introductions, directives, and peripheral commentaries by the presider. Standing during these monologues can quickly become a chore to endure until it is time to sit down and hear the scriptural readings. Here is where wise liturgical leadership can aid in proper intentionality. The liturgy begins much more powerfully and simply when it is part of the Body's summons to acknowledge together God's saving acts in Jesus: standing together we sign ourselves in the name. In this new reality as *Corpus Christi*, we praise God for God's saving acts in Jesus: "You were sent to heal the contrite of heart...." The rubrics allow for similar testimonies in the spirit of the readings. This is not a time to enter back into one's own sinfulness and thus sunder the unity of the gathered Body. We stand together under the tent of mercy, all in need, all acknowledging our identity as a sacramental Body that clings to Christ who clings to us.

Standing together, gathered as one, embodies the dignity and grace of the convocation. It is not about being "called on the carpet" regarding individual sinfulness, but about together bearing the yoke of mercy in the presence of Christ in wonder and awe. *Kyrie eleison*, the presider sings, and the assembly responds in full-bodied affirmation that, under the mercy tent, we are who we are by the grace of God's forgiving love. Beseeching is now laden with hope: "May almighty God have mercy on us, forgive us our sins, and bring us to everlasting life." The gathered Body can only pray and beg this because of the generous desire of God, who sends his Beloved to be with us, gather us, and hold us. In short, the penitential rite is about first being embraced in mercy before it is anything else.

In this light, *striking the breast* as a common gesture by the standing assembly testifies to God's saving deeds in Christ, a tactile acknowledgment of need and a shared commitment to live the truth the gathered Body represents. As Antonio Donghi says, each person's strike upon the breast is "a language" in which "there is ideally a wringing of the heart of the 'old self' in order to leave room for the new." In the context of the community gathered in grace, he says further,

> There is nothing depressing at all about this gesture: there is no discounting of the person, there is no sadness about life. Rather, the song of hope implanted by the Spirit in the heart of the believer—who now lives in the revelation of God—retraces this act of faith in the mercy of God, underlining how already in the believer's consciousness of being distant from God that person is growing in communion with God.[45]

Doing this gesture together intensifies that communion. Its communal truth enters "the skin's memory, the body's wisdom, and the geometry of prayer" because the act of liturgical anamnesis in Word and Sacrament renders present a liberating story which is now this people's own identifying truth. Hence, at the outset of this pilgrim journey, the Body

stands with and for one another as Christ's own. Christ is the corner-
stone of the geometric dimensions of this "singular vessel of devotion."
The yoke is shared. Communicating more than mere words, we stand
together to make that acknowledgment and shoulder that common
burden of our need and Christ's choice to be head and heart of this
Body. All this is played out in a gesture that, as Guardini says, "requires
of us a bearing suited to such a presence."

An added element in this poetic choreography of the penitential
rite is the particularity of *standing together in silence*. Silence among us
allows the resonance of being held to weave itself through the Body,
sheltered under the tent of mercy, communicated by a fruitful silence
in our standing together before the throne of grace. The tenor of the
rite is penitential, but it is also awesome and full of wonder. There
need to be liminal times such as this when the standing together has
no words or instructions or proclamations to accompany it. We simply
are held—together—and something settles in the sacramental Body
and prepares her to praise God in the Gloria and to sit down together
and begin to tell the story. Such an embodied attentiveness to standing
together in the penitential rite can then be liberated from its prepara-
tory orations and be the embodied prayer that a communal gesture
such as this offers.

Standing to hear and receive the Gospel seems to happen in the
Body naturally and does not need extensive justification here. It is a
universally regarded sign of respect and honor, just as when a revered
person or guest enters the room. This gesture of common esteem and
devotion for the gospel, received as word of life, can give meaning
to this gesture's role in the Eucharistic Prayer and in the reception
of Eucharist. Honor and respect on the part of the whole Body, we
can argue, coalesces around both the ambo and the table. However,
the latter postures are also areas where the most contemporary discord
abides, as if dueling theologies and expressions of devotion pull and
stretch the Body's unity and often rend the baptismal Body, leaving her
in pieces, instead of "woven in one piece from the top" (John 19:23).
Unfortunately, contemporary exhortations from those who represent
the universal Church have not helped to quell such discord.[46] From the
perspective of this meditative theology and the importance of physical
gestures as expressions of the Body's unity, how might we reflect on
the dignity and reverence of standing in a way that does not dismiss
the desire of many for solemnity and respect, as each believes is her or

his duty as a devout person of prayer? How is standing here as devout as kneeling? Can standing together announce something that is in rhythm with the iconic cadence of the eucharistic action in particular, or is it simply an idol of those who feel they are subservient to no one and no thing? Or, from the obverse perspective, can insistence on only one form of devotion be an idolatry of a gesture that is surely appropriate in some settings and not in others, an insistence of which gnaws away at the inherent value of both standing and kneeling? In this liturgical dissonance over posture, the focus turns to motive and argument that can be felt in the assembly, rather than a liberating handing over of oneself to the whole.

Certain regions of the world find value in both bodily postures at the Eucharistic Prayer. In fact, the universal General Instruction is fundamentally at odds with much North American practice. GIRM 43 states,

> The faithful should stand from the beginning of the Entrance Chant, or while the Priest approaches the altar, until the end of the Collect; for the Alleluia Chant before the Gospel; while the Gospel itself is proclaimed; during the Profession of Faith and the Universal Prayer; and from the invitation, Orate, fratres (Pray, brethren), before the Prayer over the Offerings until the end of Mass, except at the places indicated here below.

The most common adaptation of that rubric in many parts of the world is to stand at the beginning of the Preface dialogue, stand or kneel for the first part of the post-Sanctus prayer, kneel for the institutional narrative, and then stand immediately for the *mysterium fidei* acclamation until the doxology have been acclaimed. This respects a tradition where the West focused on the consecratory moment of the words of institution, a diversion from an earlier and still Eastern tradition of the consecratory focus on the epiclesis. So after a very clear directive above, the same GIRM 43 goes on to say,

> In the Dioceses of the United States of America, they should kneel beginning after the singing or recitation of the Sanctus (Holy, Holy, Holy) until after the Amen of the Eucharistic Prayer, except when prevented on occasion by ill health,

or for reasons of lack of space, of the large number of people present, or for another reasonable cause. However, those who do not kneel ought to make a profound bow when the Priest genuflects after the Consecration. The faithful kneel after the Agnus Dei (Lamb of God) unless the Diocesan Bishop determines otherwise (SC 40).

How this expresses more genuinely "the mystery of Christ and the real nature of the true Church" (SC 2) has never been expressed in a way that honors the integrity and dignity of the *primary celebrants* of the liturgy, which is the sacramental Body and not the priest presider alone. That interior attitude has been worn away through the practice of acting in the liturgy, as if the presider is doing the holy things and the faithful are called to participate with an interior acquiescence, as some documents have suggested.[47] The first thing we can assert is that gestures throughout the world and the history of liturgical practice are profoundly cultural and adaptive. Common practice may, in truth, have no theological foundation or intentional spiritual significance. It is not an adequate explanation that only a kneeling sacramental Body can give the most adequate physical expression of her devotion in these sacramental rites taking place. If that were true, the presider and con-celebrants would be encouraged to do the same. This sort of qualitative evaluation of standing versus kneeling during the Eucharistic Prayer misses the point and yields little insight into how the singular vessel of devotion might express her acclamation of faith at this sacred mystery she celebrates. Standing in some communities may precisely embody such respect and awe, given the gospel gestures mentioned above. From another perspective, kneeling may be an ingrown unworthiness to really participate, given the legacy of sinfulness and holiness in the Church tradition. But it also may not be about unworthiness. That is why the local Church needs to be in dialogue about these issues and the decisions not made by curial offices alone. Indeed, many mitigating factors, such as the size of the Church, the cultural traditions of a com-munity, and the age and ability of the congregation all play a role here. Again, the gathered assembly is the primary celebrant of the liturgy.

To make the matter more complex, it is often sadly true that a liturgical assembly is subject to the whims of a clerical or pastoral leader's own personal preference, what he thinks the faithful should do in order to respect the order each has in the hierarchy of ministry, or even what causes the least amount of tension within the Body. The argument here suggests that such ingrained or legislated attitudes can at best be questioned to see if they are in harmony with what best expresses the unity of the Body bound to Christ and Christ to them, a sacramental self-offering in praise to the Father in the matter and form of the eucharistic gifts. Here is where the leadership of the assembly, the priest who gathers the sacramental Body into communion and those who form the community's liturgical life, have a tender and focal role in shepherding the assembly in its unity, rather than hoarding them into certain gestures and positions for the sake of making clear the differences in order, rather than the wholeness of the Body herself. Indeed, after these somewhat competing expectations, the same paragraph in GIRM ends with the following dictum:

> For the sake of uniformity in gestures and bodily postures during one and the same celebration, the faithful should follow the instructions which the Deacon, a lay minister, or the Priest gives, according to what is laid down in the Missal. (no. 43; SC 40)

Clearly, there is no uniformity in the universal tradition about uniformity! And this is precisely the point. Yet, there is dis-ease in the sacramental Body when these different perspectives of devotion vie for precedence in the liturgy.

One could suggest that kneeling throughout the Eucharistic Prayer, while profoundly devotional, moves the members of the Body *at this particular point in the eucharistic celebration* away from "one Body, one Spirit in Christ" into a reengagement with personal devotion. One is reminded of Susan Wood's creative use of the work of Henri de Lubac that encourages the interrelated matrix of symbolic relationships be intensified rather than tamed into clear and separate roles of engagement. From the lens of our consideration of posture, communion involves so much more in terms of relationality and participation. Wood says,

> In terms of the Church/Eucharist correlation, the Church in union with Christ is the truth signified by the Eucharist when considered not merely in terms of the sacramental

59

species, but the entire liturgical rite within the historical matrix of memory, presence, and anticipation.[48]

Reverent devotion in this sense is not focused on an attitude directed toward the eucharistic elements alone, but that rich matrix of presence, interconnected and mutually revealing, that de Lubac labored so much in his work to make clear. The gifts of bread and wine, the blessed sacrament, are pure gifts for the Body, distinct and not separate from it. Maintaining a common gesture of standing together whenever possible and reasonable, "we are in possession of ourselves," as Guardini stated, to manifest the singular vessel of devotion. In terms of the two gestures of standing and kneeling, Guardini clarifies, "Standing is the other side of reverence toward God. Kneeling is the side of worship in rest and quietness; standing is the side of vigilance and action."[49] So the foundational principle is what is most appropriate for time and place and significance during the Eucharistic Prayer. Although kneeling may be more appropriate in a sacred space whose visual lines and configuration may commend it, standing is certainly the most intentionally significant gesture when the architectural lines allow. It is not the lesser gesture of devotion. "Standing is the other side of reverence." As complex as such decisions for the good of the Body are, the symbolic role of the assembly "praying and singing" (SC 7) weighs in here as the primary criterion, and not some sense that what is happening at the altar is embodied as both distinct *and* separate from the sacramental Body who is the primary celebrant. Communities need to be honest about this.

Handing over idols to which we cling—for whatever reason—and receiving the appropriate iconic gesture that is most expressive and appropriate in *this* time and place, for *these* people, allows both gestures of standing or kneeling to function iconically in this "poem of thanksgiving." As we noted from St. Paul, the Spirit animates the grace that hallows and draws together this Body, "and where the Spirit of the Lord is, there is freedom" (2 Cor 3:17). The presider gathers that Body into communion and represents Christ as Head and heart, but only in dialogical, relational, and participative communion with the assembly.[50] Indeed, as Guardini insists elsewhere, the individual finds her or his true identity in clinging to this communion:

The individual is made aware of the unity which comprehends him on many and various occasions, but chiefly in the liturgy. In it he sees himself face to face with God, *not as an entity, but as a member of this unity.* It is the unity which addresses God; the individual merely speaks in it, and it is *required of him that he should know and acknowledge that he is a member of it.*[51]

Standing together, therefore, is a venerable and traditional mode of Christian prayer, as A. G. Martimort noted in his classic treatise on *Principles of the Liturgy*, part of the rich collection of liturgical scholarship emerging from the Council. He describes the painting and art depicting this in the early catacombs, sarcophaguses, and mosaics. He notes that when the orations are given voice by the celebrant—clearly an embodied expression of *ecclesia orans*—the whole body stands. He concludes that this is "the characteristic paschal posture," held as primary in the East today and obligatory during the Easter season, which St. Irenaeus called "a symbol of the resurrection." He illumines this from an interior attitude of freedom and profound trust in the redemptive acts of God in Christ, much as we have insisted throughout this exploration:

Standing is also the proper posture of those who await the blessed parousia: in the presence of God only they remain standing who have nothing to fear of his justice (Mal 3:2); the Hebrews in Egypt probably stood as they ate the Passover in haste, always ready to set out (Exod 12:11); finally, the elect stand in heaven as they give thanks (Rev. 7:9, 15:2).[52]

This communal, upright posture of the faithful before the throne of grace is not the figment of progressive liturgical imagination or willfulness, and so it deserves its place within contemporary tradition as well. It is "traditional" and "orthodox" in the best sense of the terms.

Such an honorable gesture is so transparent when the assembly and ministers are incensed at solemn celebrations. The presider incenses the holy things (altar, crucifix, paschal candle, etc.) and then hands the thurible to the minister who will incense the ministers and assembly. If choreographed with intentionality and care, the thurifer bows and the one incensed bows in response and acclamation. Matter and form "effect the grace they signify" if she or he moves around to different parts of the assembly, bids them to stand and bow in a mutual act of reverence, and then moves to include more and more of the assembly so that the wholeness of the Body is orchestrated before our eyes is a resonant "poem of thanksgiving." The ritual cadence is physical and geometrical and visually builds upon the unity of the assembly precisely in the movement of a community unfolding in her unity as she is "gathered from the four winds" to become the sacramental event of the Body praying. The exhortation upon completion, "Pray, brothers and sisters, that my sacrifice and yours may be acceptable to God, the almighty Father," rings out with greater clarity when accompanied by this bodily gesture of the assembly. The communal response, "May the Lord accept the sacrifice at your hands for the praise and glory of his name, for our good and the good of all his holy church," makes the impending self-offering of the sacramental Body in union with Christ and the offering of the firstfruits of bread and wine true and mystical, an embodied expression of "our duty and our salvation, always and everywhere to give you thanks." Here acknowledged gift is received and now to be offered back "through Christ our Lord," *per ipsum, et cum ipso, et in ipso*. The inside and the outside sing a single song of praise.

What then can we conclude from this and many similar liturgical moments communicated within a uniformity of matter and form? Given an attentive intentionality to the recovery of the sacramental Body's focal role in that matrix of symbolic relationships, and honoring the place that bodily gesture and movement play in the manifestation of the unity of the Body of Christ, interior and exterior, Head and members, mind and body and spirit, such gestures when standing together should be affirmed and encouraged whenever possible and the cultural and spatial conditions commend it. Such a stance is not over and against kneeling in terms of a pious act of devotion, but both represent part of the cadence and rhythm of a liturgical assembly with many faces and emotions and seasons of celebration. It is to the particularity of kneeling that we now turn.

Kneeling together can then be given its proper honor and role as a *communal* posture of devotion when seen as a complementary gesture with standing. Contemporary practice certainly has never dismissed kneeling, but over the centuries it was embodied in such a way as an expression of one's personal attitude and feeling and not that of the sacramental Body as a singular vessel. However, this does not diminish its rich importance as a devotional, though not always communal, posture for prayer. To this end, kneeling expresses a variety of interior attitudes in communion with Christ and one's sisters and brothers in faith. Certainly, and Dalmais notes them, kneeling is "a sign of mourning, humility, and repentance." It is also an expression of "private prayer" alone or before the community that one embodies in meditation or as preparation for mission and vowed commitment. Scriptural examples are most notably Stephen before his martyrdom (Acts 7:60), Paul and the community before setting out on a voyage (Acts 21:5), and Peter in preparation for apostolic ministry of prayer and healing (Acts 9:40). Much later in the Western tradition, Dalmais notes the growing movement toward "periods of prayer on one's knees when adoring the Eucharist and receiving communion." He highlights the importance of all these situations in the present reform except, importantly, kneeling to receive communion, since "the posture did not allow the faithful to come to Communion in procession, and it is hardly compatible with Communion in the hand."[53]

Arguments of taste and temperament abound here. However, as a *liturgical* gesture of a praying Body clinging to Christ and one another, a rich expression of unity can unfold through kneeling. Some examples may assist our ritual imaginations here. When a servant of the community kneels before the assembly, it is an individual gesture with communal significance. It reflects the covenant to serve or is asking forgiveness of both God and the community in time of institutional or personal misdeeds. Kneeling before a standing community gathered around evokes the prayer and anointing of the Holy Spirit that is flowing in and through the assembly as a mystical Body and a true presence of Christ. This freely offered sign of "mourning, humility, and repentance" is profoundly liturgical and covenantal and communicates so much more than words of vows, contrition, or need for hallowing could ever adequately convey.

Times of communal penance and adoration that call for meditation on the awesome holiness of God or express a deeper intimacy with the kenosis of Christ also beg for kneeling by the whole Body. Like the gesture of prostration on Good Friday and at ordinations, it suggests surrender in a special way of one's whole self, an act of humility resplendent in dignity, because it bodies forth Christ.[54] Seen from this perspective, kneeling together—and accompanying silence seems to be a rich collaborator in this movement and gesture—is a deep source of unity. Benediction is a very poignant example, especially when done in the midst of the Liturgy of the Hours. Accompanied by standing and bowing in the recitation of the psalms of vespers on Sunday, for example, and then the whole community's turn to the altar toward the exposition of the blessed sacrament, kneeling communicates in bodily form a profoundly communal and grace-full nourishment for the soul of the sacramental Body.

The efficacy of this communal gesture is so powerful the more the assembly acknowledges this unity with intentional attention and with patterned regularity. Something happens in ways that cooperate with the complementary grace of standing together in the liturgy, together communicating a freedom and dignity and a willingness to be sent. Together—and not in competition or expressed by individual choice—they body forth the same bonding and grace, what Guardini called "a bearing suited to the presence." In fact, a sustained, communal rubric of kneeling seems to cry out for the community to stand and sing a prayer of praise and accept the mission that this prayer exacted together expresses. *Kneeling together* and *standing together*, and also bowing and striking the breast, lifting up hands "like the evening sacrifice," and other suitable gestures, can then work together like the elements of a poem. Each has its dignified place, and each honors the other so that this matrix of symbolic relationships brings harmony to the whole. Would not our liturgy wars profit from a perspective that honors such a poetics? Would it not allow flexibility, creativity, and diverse expressions to shape the unity of the Body to shine forth as the iconic singular vessel of devotion she is called to be? One is reminded at the end of this discussion of Paul's warning about belonging to one camp of Apollos or of Paul as a form of thinking disembodied from the whole: "What then is Apollos? What is Paul? Servants through whom you came to believe, as the Lord assigned to each. I planted, Apollos watered, but God gave the growth" (1 Cor 3:5–6).

The unity of the Body gathered in the name of the trinitarian communion suggests this is possible and that the wholeness and integrity of the Body has room for diversity within unity. In that light, assemblies where individuals stand when others kneel, or who kneel when others stand, say more about the tears in the whole garment rather than the wholeness of the tunic. Leadership, as we said,

64

is crucial here, but leadership needs a kenotic honesty, courage, and discernment in addressing the tear. The gestures of the assembly *are* important. They *matter* and *form*. The yoke of leadership must seek the attitude of Christ the Head so that the *totus Christus* can offer praise and thanks and adoration that is "truly right and just."

Finally, *processing together* gives bodily expression to communal identity and devotion by means of a choreographed rhythm that only becomes conducive for the singular vessel of devotion praying when it is introduced over time, practiced with a patterned regularity, and orchestrated to facilitate the movement of bodies together gracefully. It is the liturgical pilgrimage within the context of *lo cotidiano*, which manifests the spiritual journey in ways that reveal more than this specific moment or this particular assembly and space can contain. Within the "geometry of prayer," it is rooted in this most archetypal expression of the inexhaustible richness of creation's continual movement toward the new Eden and the eternal home for which she longs.

Antonio Donghi describes the beautiful rhythm and cadence of communal procession as a bodily gesture expressing an interior unity of praying for the sacramental Body:

> The liturgical celebration involves processional gestures, for the procession of the people of God and the ministers parallels our continuous walk toward the eternal pastures of the kingdom. In this gesture, we proclaim that we have here no fixed home, that we do not depend on any stability, since we know that life in all its meanings and relationships moves ever forward, that life is always in motion. Walking signifies life itself—searching, looking, deciding, departing toward that which gives meaning to existence. Such behavior is more than locomotion; it suggests the very meaning of life.[55]

Because procession by its very nature is inimical to passivity and requires bodies to rise and join together and move in step, reverent procession must be intentionally attentive to many things and set in motion by leaders who welcome the participation and monitor its cadence. It is not simply a vehicle to get from one place to another. Indeed, most of the time it circles and winds its way through a very limited space rather than the obvious destination of a spiritual pilgrimage from one holy shrine to another. The entrance procession, for example, makes its way through the assembled Body, drawing the whole assembly into a communal attitude that gives outward expression to an interior intention:

> Enter his gates with thanksgiving
>> and his courts with praise.
> Give thanks to him, bless his name. (Ps 100:4)

So many tender examples describe this. The sacramental Body processes with the remains of a loved one who has died, all following the thurible or processional cross or paschal candle as an expression of the entrance at long last into the fullness of life. She processes with palms and sings Hosanna, to bind herself more closely to the Lord's triumphant entrance into Jerusalem on Palm Sunday. She carries the fragments of her Eucharist to the altar of repose and walks with the solemnity of the Lord himself as he enters into the final drama of his redeeming death. And when she reaches what is fittingly called the "altar of repose," she pauses there with him, as in the garden on the night before he died, and makes vigil before she departs in silence to continue the procession to the cross on the following day in adoration and loving memory. The Great Vigil continues that journey from the Easter fire into the darkened Church, now emblazoned by the lights of the those who pass the light as they move from the outside into the inside. The sacramental Body processing to communion, each member opening her hands in surrender to receive the gift and consume and commune, is an activity whose richness as a single act of the *Corpus Christi* gives visual expression to the grace of "communion incarnate." The assembly who processes into the streets of the neighborhood and secular boundaries of life is a powerful liturgical symbol of the cosmic dimensions of a faith in a God who desires that all may come into the embrace and dignity of their lives, and especially their lives together. Processing, we can unequivocally assert, is very holy. Its significance spills over from the liturgy into the lives of all who walk in solidarity of faith, walk for freedom, raising a communal voice of protest over injustice, expressing grief, celebrating victory, or honoring those the community raises up. Processing together, we could say, has a liturgical language uniquely its own.

All this being said, processing in a contemporary Western culture with its sense of individuality is not easy. It requires a kenosis on the part of the isolated individual who walks the hard road of life alone, dramatically proclaiming a new identity within the faith community that, as Donghi said, "suggests the meaning of life." We are bound to Christ and one another, and he to us. It testifies to a faith that we often do not wear on our sleeves in the quotidian pattern of everyday movement, often a frenetic pacing to and fro with no apparent meaning or direction. The secular world, often unfamiliar and perhaps even hostile toward such public displays of faith, is arrested and nudged to wonder who these people walking together are and why they need to do it together. A devotional procession, with a humble dignity, "speaks" volumes through the vessel of the walking Body.

These processions should be more frequent, so that what seems at first an awkward cadence can gradually inscribe itself on the worshiping assembly and the focused intent can shift to the Body praying as she moves. Donghi does not take this prayerful aspect lightly: "To walk is to pray, to search, to thirst for an identity, to long for authentic human relationship."[56] Through that praying with the Body we come to know as persons that we are truly held by Christ and by the sisters and brothers to whom we are bound in "communion incarnate." Pope Francis has captured the simplicity of this "belonging" as an ecclesial act:

> I think this is truly the most wonderful experience we can have: to belong to a people walking, journeying through history together with our Lord, who walks among us! We are not alone; we do not walk alone. We are part of the one flock of Christ that walks together.[57]

Perhaps this is why the spiritual pilgrimage, such as Santiago de Compostela and the labyrinth walk as a communal spiritual practice, is so appealing to contemporary seekers and believers, particularly the young. This is a gesture and a movement that invites harmony with many other sacramental expressions of a people's faith, such as the procession with the paschal candle as the pillar of fire leading the people out of slavery into freedom, or the sweet allure of incense that wafts around and through everyone and everything as a hallowing in the Spirit that is alive, moving, and "blowing where she will." There is "plenty good room" in the makeup of this pilgrimage: icons of biblical stories carried in the procession that the community now claims as her story, the devotional images of holy women and men, young people very much alive and part of this Body as a "new creation" in their communion attire, and servers with torches who signal the arrival of the bridegroom for whom we all await, accompanied by chanting that comes from the soul and not from a complicated text, bells and drums and even rhythmic steps—there is a spacious tent in this bodily movement and gesture to house all of these in a procession. Together they speak of redemption, liberation, faithful shepherding, companionship along the way, and the grace of simply carrying on, placing one foot before another. Processing together should never lose its place in our ritual lives, but it also does not happen without intentionality and regularity and a willingness to let go of the vanities of sophistication and self-focus to which we often cling so tenaciously. As Donghi says so eloquently,

> To learn to walk is to learn to grow in the sense of life and to give flesh to the joy of living that will enable us to walk eternally in the presence of the Holy Trinity. In the liturgy we pass continually from time to eternity, wrapped up in the paschal mystery and pressed by the Spirit. This is our processional walking in the liturgical assembly.[58]

Processing together, therefore, is worth the exercise and practice it requires to express the richness of "communion incarnate." It embodies what Evdokimov proclaimed as the "one true attitude of the human soul" that Mary represents as the *Orant*, that we "*be* prayer, prayer incarnate...a hymn of adoration, an offering, a prayer."[59] In giving poetic expression in Psalm 42 of his interior longing and thirst for God, wondering when that fullness that now seems so distant may at last draw near, the Psalmist exclaims hope in the midst of a life journey so familiar to all of us, which the community embraces in anamnesis at worship:

> These things I remember
>   as I pour out my soul:
> how I went with the throng,
>   and led them in procession to the house of God,
> with glad shouts and songs of thanksgiving,
>   a multitude keeping festival. (Ps 42:4)

SOME CONCLUSIONS: HOLDING MOVEMENT AND GESTURE IN POETIC TENSION IN THE TRUE AND MYSTICAL BODY AT PRAYER

The gestures and movements characteristic of the "true and mystical Body" have been explored in this chapter as a revelatory, kinetic embodiment of her interior attitude, united to the mind and heart of Christ, outlined in chapter 1. We return again to the importance of maintaining the tension inherent in an ambiguity of the *Corpus Christi* that is intentional and significant, to borrow again Henri de Lubac's helpful categories. One can suspect that de Lubac's retrenchment that occurred later in his life regarding the liturgical reforms of Vatican II may have been a reaction to the temptation from both progressive and conservative perspectives to squeeze the life out of that generative tension. To explain away the sacred mysteries with mind-numbing commentaries and relevant triviality in music or vesture on the one extreme, or to isolate the eucharistic species from the mystical Body of Christ on the other, so that even the reception of communion is considered secondary to the miraculous changes happening on the altar, destroys the poetic grace of what de Lubac called "the real continuity that exists between head and members of the unique body...(and) the symbolic bond between the sacrament and the community."[60]

That is why this chapter added the contemporary work of others such as Dalmais, Mitchell, Chauvet, and Lafont, who spoke of the liturgy and its expression as, to use the latter's term, a "poem of thanksgiving." The rhythm and harmony of the liturgy as an embodied poetic poem highlights the specific importance of the *matter* and *form* employed to sing God's praises, just like word and cadence *matter* and *form* any poem. They express "the skin's memory, the body's wisdom, and the geometry of prayer," as Mitchell called it. The liturgical poem, rooted in the very real and specific, speaks a truth that cannot be captured in a linear logic that both extremes of the liturgical spectrum labor to employ. "Its language," Lafont said, "is unique, at once human and surpassing what is human."[61] Without the creative tension, its liturgical "sprung rhythm,"[62] between real bodies and holy things accompanied

69

by a strange yoking together of meanings and purpose (e.g., the paschal candle *is* a pillar of fire on many levels and the baptismal font *is* a womb and also a tomb), the sacramental Body atrophies. When the poetic nature of the sacramental Body is not honored, liturgical experts and separate "orders" take over more and more and minimalize the bare bones that are left so that the "symbolic bond" is fragile at best. This chapter has insisted on the puzzling and awesome grace: "*This* is my Body." This is Christ's Body. This is the eucharistic Body. This is the sacramental Body. This is the Church convoked in prayer who manifests to others "the mystery of Christ and the true nature of the Church" (SC 2). To mine the riches of de Lubac on this intentional ambiguity and liturgical poetics one more time, he says,

> As long as the world lasts, we are still living "*in the sacraments*," that is to say, explains St. Gregory of Great, not yet in our permanent home, but hovering on the threshold, "*between doors*." Our Passover from now on is Christ, but it is always taking us further. And in the providential diversity of their forms, without it ever being possible to separate their "spiritual" and the "bodily" aspects, are not all the means of salvation at the same time, according to *whether we see them from within or from outside*, and relation to a sterile past or to a good anticipated, an image, that is to say simultaneously both figure and truth?[63]

So we need to allow the sacramental Body to "hover" there in creative tension. This is the "True and Mystical Body" who needs a body to be a Body, and who needs the poetry of gesture and movement to sign and name the christic form and matter through, with, and in whom they gather through the hallowing of the Holy Spirit as agent and bond. In this trinitarian matrix in which the liturgical assembly is embedded, all praise now returns to the pierced heart of the Father, the source of any devotion: "for we belong to the Body and the Body belongs to Christ, and Christ belongs to God" (cf. 1 Cor 3:23). A final vignette of "communion incarnate" will end the chapter.

At the Solemn Vespers of Pentecost, the last of the Easter season, the community of a cathedral in Seattle, Washington, gathers to chant the Psalms antiphonally and celebrate Benediction. But the opening procession on this special day of festive ending begins with the community

70

accompanying the white-clad neophytes to the font one more time to bring the paschal candle to its future home in "Ordinary Time." Gathered around the font, the presider tells the sacramental Body gathered there with the neophytes in their embrace, "We bring the paschal candle to the baptistery at the entrance to the Church because here is where it will live for the rest of the year. It will greet all who enter and bathe in the font, and it will welcome our beloved dead; it will be a sign of Christ's Body, who lives here." And then turning to the neophytes, he tells them, "This is where you began, where you were reborn with us. You have worn these distinguishing garments for fifty days, and now it is time to take them off. The figurative color of all your clothing now is red, as I am wearing, because you are now on mission." The candle "lives" and has a home. The neophytes are now members of the Body, having been clothed and nurtured as if they were children, but dressed now, "geared and ready for action," as Guardini said. They are wed now to this Body, the bride of Christ, to its work of evangelization, in order to share their gifts with her, as Paul says, as those "equipped as saints"

> for the work of ministry, for building up the body of Christ, until all of us come to the unity of the faith and of the knowledge of the Son of God, to maturity, to the measure of the full stature of Christ (Eph 4:12–13).

They are unique persons with distinct stories, but now they are marked with the sign of the cross on their bodies in the midst of this Body. They are part of the "already" and "not yet." The end of the season is the beginning of the new reality within the context of *lo cotidiano.* Then the procession makes its pilgrimage back up the aisle, to do the work of its chanting and prayer and communal adoration. This cannot be conveyed in its richness by words alone. One must be there and "do this in memory of Me."

When the liturgy is celebrated with such intentional attention, all seems true and real, in rhythm and harmony, and very holy in every last matter and form. We now move in the next chapter to voice and word, which gives its own unique timbre to the song of the singular vessel of devotion.

Chapter 3

A Voice and an Ear to Sing God's Praise

The Resonance of Sacred Speech in the Sacramental Body

Son is the word for the Word
of the beginning begot.

Ballad I: "In Principio," *The Poems of John of the Cross*[1]

Bodies communicate in many ways, and each body's voice has a special rhythm and harmony that communicates through word and sound and accompanying bodily gesture what is in the heart and mind and soul. "For it is out of the abundance of the heart that the mouth speaks," as Jesus instructs the disciples in Luke 6:45. A person's verbal speech, therefore, is not a reality complete unto itself. It is saying *something to someone*, even if that other is one's own self or a mysterious transcendent Presence one believes to be beyond the self. By its nature, the voice suggests communication, conversation, relationality, and the necessary response component of active listening to another to complete the interchange. The voice and the ear are intimate partners in the communication of the heart.

The dynamism, dialogue, and participation that make up speech conspire together to take part in making the human voice a vehicle of identity, mutuality, and creativity—and even prophetic action.[2] We use the description that when a person speaks, what one says and how it is said "sounds like *you*" or "does *not* sound like you." Human speech and song reveal integrity and an interior/exterior resonance with what the voice utters and who the hearer experiences the person to be and feel and believe. Truly, voice and speech make up a complex "matrix of symbolic relationships." Verbal communication is also part of a poetic discourse on many other levels because what the voice is saying is not limited to the words alone. Body language, for example, is part of this creative and mysterious communication we call language, and so, when the body communicates, more is being said than the objective meaning of the words alone. The phrase "All of this is a roundabout way of saying…" is a familiar indicator of our awareness that there is more to speech than meets the ear or the eye. The unique tone and emphasis the voice gives to each word also play a role and add to the mix of meaning. Without a doubt, the resonance in speech is multidimensional.

In the communication event, all these characteristics are at play, especially when the word to be communicated is foundational and vital to the conversation. "What you say speaks volumes" is the adage. Considering the realm of sacred speech and communal word, this is especially true and deserves closer scrutiny. The *sensus plenior* aspect of Scripture—that there is a deeper and always revelatory character to what is written or said—holds true for all ritual speech communication.[3] From a sacramental perspective, this should give us pause to wonder about the mystery of voice and speech in communicating what is true and real and holy, and also how voice and word are heard and "effect the reality that they signify." This rich field of spiritual conversation takes place within the context of *lo cotidiano*, in what is most ordinary in matter and form, but *precisely* in that ordinariness can convey an interior attitude and depth that proclaim something that may be truly extraordinary. So much is going on in the body that speaks about important and identity-making things.

THE SACRAMENTAL BODY SPEAKING AND HEARING: ENTERING THE TRINITARIAN CONVERSATION

The transcendence communicated in the midst of what is most ordinary exhibits special characteristics and resonance within the sacramental Body as a singular vessel of devotion, whose prayerful utterances, communal reading, and body language and posture are an essential part of the harmony and wholeness of the unity of Head and members. As promised in the introduction, the discussion now will explore the quality of the sacramental voice of this Body at prayer, how she speaks as one Body united with her Lord and bound to the sisters and brothers in faith. We will examine how such voice acts of proclamation and preaching and interceding before God, evoking and expressing praise and lament, have a sweet timbre and resonance and, indeed, their own poetic cadence. Ghislain Lafont speaks to this mellifluous harmony of voices as *a* voice that invokes an "epiphany of life" that is "recalling a past and wishing a future." He goes on to describe this interchange:

> Discourse is, first of all, voice; it is song; it is music. But it is a voice for someone else, it addresses another and utters a proper name. Sometimes it is pronounced in the name of others. And so it begins to tell of something. Within an already established communion, it evokes, it remembers, it also anticipates.[4]

Thus the "established communion" of a sacramental Body in festal gathering has a unique voice and a particular poetic rhythm, whose revelatory speech is most transparent, not in a cacophony of competing voices, but in a diverse yet still unified voice that proclaims from the heart of many the liturgical song now voiced as one.

What is more, part of the rhythmic harmony of the sacramental Body means that she first listens attentively to the sacred Word that she herself speaks and then, within her own voice, gives expression to its divine resonance in her heart and soul and mind. In this marvelous exchange, the ear and the voice are intimate partners in symbolic communication that harmonizes the inside and the outside. And so the voice acts are simply part of a fuller proclamation taking place as the "one whole Word of God,"[5] to which the liturgy gives privileged expression on so many levels of bodily expression. First John gives us a glimpse into the power of that multivalent sensual testimony:

> We declare to you what was from the beginning, what we have heard, what we have seen with our eyes, what we have looked at and touched with our hands, concerning the word of life—this life was revealed, and we have seen it and testify to it, and declare to you the eternal life that was with the Father and was revealed to us—we declare to you what we have seen and heard so that you also may have fellowship with us; and truly our fellowship is with the Father and with his Son Jesus Christ. (1 John 1:1–3)

The voice of the sacramental Body never speaks for its own edification or entertainment; it is not concerned with what we would call idle (or idol) chatter.[6] It is about true and real communion, holy communion, "communion incarnate," as we have named it in the previous chapter. The source of the voice in the Body is holy and is its wellspring. The character of its role as a sacramental vehicle is rooted in the Creator whose heart is pierced in love and is communicated in the Word who gives birth to that incarnate embrace, which the Spirit circulates through the gathered community of faith to say something new. St. John of the Cross's simple poetic words at the outset of this chapter "speak volumes" here: "Son is the word for the Word / of the beginning begot." The embodied Word that resonates within the Body—which is her true voice—is given as a gratuitous gift of the Trinity's own communion. The response of the Body is to utter thanks and praise "with one heart and mind and voice." In the introduction, we made a similar point with John's harmonic beginning of his Gospel: "In the beginning was the Word, and the Word was with God, and the Word was God" (1:1). We called it a spiritual journal of a divine relationship that is now the icon of Christ's devotion shared with the sacramental Body who gathers in his name. Truly, the liturgical community is a privileged, uttered expression of the faithful's identity as "people of the word."

It is important not to forget these divine origins of something so ordinary and quotidian as speaking and listening and sharing conversation, especially in the context of this most profound manifestation we call the liturgy.[7] The twentieth-century Dominican theologian Herbert McCabe highlights the mutuality of human communication to, for, and about God. It is endemic to the nature of human persons and to the living communion incarnate in the *Corpus Christi*, Head and members, to be bound together in a grace-filled unity. This divine communication between Head and members, part of the redemptive dialogue between Father and Son,[8] enables her to have a graceful voice as the Spirit-filled, resurrected Body of Christ present in the world. McCabe says,

> We are creatures who are on speaking terms with God. Because of the divine life in us, the Spirit of God in us, we are able to listen to what God says—this is what we call faith. Because of the divine life in us, we are able to speak back to God.[9]

The trinitarian heart of liturgical communication is articulated beautifully here because it is rooted in the Father, given filial and bodily expression in the Son, and animated in sacred speech to which only the Holy Spirit can give adequate expression within the sacramental Body.

So the body's common voice, the words that are spoken, and the ears that hear and receive what is expressed are crucial dimensions of a liturgical assembly that expresses itself in the mind and heart of Christ. The singular vessel in its common prayer joins its voice with Christ's to acknowledge God's saving acts by means of the narrative of invocation, evocation, praise and storytelling, chanting and singing, to name just a few aspects of the communal voice and her devotion. Ghislain Lafont ponders the rich characteristics of this mode of communication. He asks a question important for this activity of the "communion incarnate" invoking and evoking God in liturgy when he describes the addressed and exchanged word as "an epiphany of life...and from the mouth there comes forth a word of joy and remembrance." He notes, "Is such a discourse—invocation and evocation—just a fleeting rite, or does it actually carry life within itself? And who knows, does it contain something of eternity?"[10] The resonance of the human voice as a bearer of divine life participates in God's graceful utterance. It is only because of this dynamic union that signifies the very communion of the sacramental Body itself that John can utter the great mystery of faith at the beginning of his narrative story of life with God in Jesus: "And the Word became flesh and lived [pitched his tent] among us, and we have seen his glory, the glory as of a father's only son, full of grace and truth" (John 1:14).[11] At the same time, the sacramental Body's auditory voice—just as for the individual human body—always is embedded in a matrix of symbolic relationships. Ritual speech employs a liturgical "body language" that is continually saying more than what is linear or logical, and it expresses itself most clearly in the intentional ambiguity of symbolic communication embodied in real people and real time, in every place and season. Indeed, the Word pitched his tent among us, and that in itself tells us much about the voice of the Lord we serve and seek to follow and to stay where he stays. It has its own stresses and accents, its own "sprung rhythm," as we noted in the previous chapter concerning Gerard Manley Hopkins's particular way of making poetry.[12] It is the assembly's way of entering into the trinitarian conversation.

THE DISTINCTIVE RESONANCE OF MANY VOICES AS ONE VOICE

What, then, are the characteristics of this sacramental discourse? How does the liturgical assembly speaking in one voice articulate the stresses and accents peculiar to this Body's "poem of thanksgiving"? The timbre and quality of sound are enriched when each individual member joins the gathered assembly to pray and sing together. At first glance, vocal prayer that is communal seems so simple. The temptation is to think of this activity merely as a recitation or chant of a rubrical or scriptural text or lyric, whose meaning at face value is the primary focus of the action, and all individually join in to say the same thing together. Truly, as we will see further, the proper prayers of the presider and the vocal prayers of the assembly and their common hymns do carry the resonance of a rich tradition of faith now put into words or song to express an ongoing identity with the communion of saints past and present. The cadence of participation takes place precisely within this enactment here and now, articulated and verified in specific words and ritual patterns associated with what has been passed down in the *mysterium fidei*. From the perspective of the sacramental Body as a singular vessel of devotion, the eventful act of praying and singing in one voice is a primary theological act in itself, where we can truly say that Christ is sacramentally present, as the Constitution on the Sacred Liturgy notes so unambiguously. SC 7 says,

> [Christ] is present in His word, since it is He Himself who speaks when the holy scriptures are read in the Church. He is present, lastly, when the Church prays and sings, for He promised: "Where two or three are gathered together in my name, there am I in the midst of them" (Matt 18:20).

Notice that the presence of Christ in word and assembly is not a static one but is revelatory and given its shape and voice when the Scriptures "are *read* in the Church" and "when the Church *prays and sings*."

So the voice of the Body here—and this is a great mystery of faith—*is* the voice of Christ now speaking as Head and heart of the communion of voices that together shares the tasks of sacred speech: of *reading* the narrative and *responding* together to its power to save; by *expressing* praise and thanks, lament and desire, through invocation and evocation, narrative prayer and song; and by means of other "accents and stresses" of gestures and postures, taking form in diverse liturgical roles of members chosen to be the assembly's voice at various times, all of which together compose a sacramental discourse that acknowledges the covenantal bond of this Body. When we *do* this, the tradition says, "This is my Body" in a very real and life-giving way. Since this is a shared conversation between God and the assembly, the members among themselves, and the Church with the world, the listening ear begins to expect a word of grace from its wellspring, to receive it in faith, and to give voice to what the ear hears. As the action of a Body in unison, A. G. Martimort says, the members are invited to "periods of more intense prayer,"[13] that rise up out of the very moment of utterance, whether in joy and praise, but also in petition, lament, and sure hope. "Let us hold fast to the confession of our hope without wavering," the Letter to the Hebrews says, "for he who has promised is faithful" (Heb 10:23). In the deepening engagement of this spiritual conversation, the sacramental Body is lending her voice to the "dialogue between God and [God's] people." As the dedication prayer of a new lectern in the holy house where the Church dwells describes so eloquently,

> May the word of God resound always in this building,
> to open for you the mystery of Christ
> and to bring about your salvation in the Church.[14]

That mystery is unfolding in the speaking, and the common voice within the rite announces the salvific acts of God in Jesus, to whom we are bound, Head and members, in the power of the Spirit. The Body of Christ is now embraced by "the word for the Word / of the beginning begot," as John of the Cross's poem tries to bring a symbolic meaning to what is happening both inside and outside the Body at prayer. There is so much resonance to the mystery of Christ when "one Body, one Spirit in Christ" uses her one voice to sing God's praise.

THE BODY'S VOICE AS REVELATORY VEHICLE FOR GOD'S SAVING ACTS IN JESUS

Rich scholarship has developed throughout history to speak of the role of Scripture and common prayer in the liturgical tradition. Part of the dynamism of the mid-twentieth century *ressourcement* movement to return to the sources of our ecclesial tradition was to bring to light how age after age, from early accounts such as the *Apostolic Tradition*, the Didache, and others, and continuing on in the patristic and medieval prayers and devotional hymns, and down to the present, the voice of God is alive and actively speaking in the Church's common worship. That dynamism is now given a present voice in the contemporary liturgical Body.

Employing different cultural contexts and theological worldviews throughout this span of ecclesial history, the use of Scriptures and sacred speech in the liturgy has been a rich narrative of a people struggling to allow this revelatory word a space to be heard in her prayer and belief and mission. The work of spiritual writers and theologians provides an excellent resource for uncovering the different ways the voice of the sacramental Body has become communion incarnate in every time and season.[15] What can be helpful in terms of this present exploration is to appreciate how the unity of the sacramental Body is deepened and enhanced when an attentive intentionality and an appreciative reverence for the power of the proclaimed word is given its due place in the actions of the universal ecclesial voice emerging from a diversity of cultural and theological horizons. These voices throughout the liturgical tradition "sound like us" who are now handing ourselves over to be held by him and holding him in grateful memory. Each age, each local community, united by her pastors, embodies the revelatory vehicle for proclaiming that saving encounter.

How then do God's saving acts in history, incarnate now in Christ as Head of this Body, find particular and concrete expression through the speech acts of the liturgical assembly? We will look at (1) proclamation and response as invocative and evocative, (2) the communal reading of sacred texts, (3) the body language that gives stress and accent to the voice, (4) the voice of the presider as an ecclesial voice in prayer and preaching, (5) active listening and silence on the part of all as crucial in this dialogue, and (6) the particular richness of music and singing as a proclamation of the Body's communion incarnate. Together these dimensions of voice say something about God's uttered Word of grace to us, for us, and in us. When this redemptive dialogue is given room to breathe in and breathe out, a powerful communication is taking place.[16] Clement of Alexandria's second-century insight into this dynamic is a rich image for this eventful speech the living Body undertakes in prayer. He says, "Breathing together is properly said of the Church. For the sacrifice of the church is the word breathing as incense from holy souls, the sacrifice and the whole mind being at the same time unveiled in God" (*Stromata*, VII.6). The sacrifice of which Clement speaks is the handing over of the individual believers into the dimension of the covenantal Body, united as Head and members. It expresses the unity of the inside with the outside, together bodying forth its true identity, "unveiled in God." Once again, in the voice at prayer, we can say with deep awe, "*This* is my Body."

(1) *Proclamation and response as invocative and evocative*—Ghislain Lafont's insistence on the dynamism of liturgical speaking as "an epiphany of life" speaks to the importance of both proclaiming God "with force and tenderness" and then, in a further revelation of this sacred speech, the Body responds to the invocation of love that occasioned this speech and she is now inspired (in the best sense of that term) to say more and be more together through the Holy Spirit's hallowing. The Body's prayerful voice enters the conversation: "We praise you; we bless you; we glorify you. We believe." This memorial "evocation" gathers God's saving deeds into the present and makes their utterance life-giving speech and, as Lafont says, "its *raison d'être*" for the festal gathering in faith.[17]

Invocation and evocation: the dialogical pattern is intentional, giving shape to the inside and outside of the Body through whom this voice resonates. The structure of liturgical praying takes this shape: you—who—do—through—amen. We acknowledge that God's redemptive acts in history have been announced to us through Word and Sacrament. The words the Body uses in her celebration gives flesh to the Church's sharing in the saving acts of Jesus, now moving in them through the power of the Spirit, and so she responds, "Amen—so be it." This is the reason why liturgy in its basic rhythm is proclamation and response, breathing in and breathing out, never a one-way monologue, but a spiritual conversation between loving partners that in itself speaks volumes and whose plenitude is never exhausted. "Let us give thanks to the Lord our God," the Preface dialogue says, and the Body responds, "It is right and just."

It *is* truly right and just, always and in every place, to use this dynamism of the Preface structure, to let God's voice be heard in the holy place and for the sacramental Body to hear it communally, to acknowledge its saving power, and to affirm its sure hope and promise as Christ's own word. The voices intermingle, God and humanity, with the angels and saints, and the faithful assembly now conspires to articulate the Word made flesh, who has pitched his tent among us. It is such a commingling of divine Word with sacred speech to which the Body gives voice. This is, we could say, why Lafont calls liturgical speaking an "epiphany" and what St. Paul calls in the Letter to the Hebrews "living and active" (Heb 4:12) that truly cuts to the marrow and bone of this Body and gives it matter and form as a sacramental Body. It effects a new hearing for this time and place and people.

> Let all the nations gather together,
>> and let the peoples assemble.
> Who among them declared this,
>> and foretold to us the former things?
> Let them bring their witnesses to justify them,
>> and let them hear and say, "It is true." (Isa 43:9)

We conclude, therefore, that the sacramental Body's voice in the liturgy is a dialogical speech act at its core and not a verbal rubric passively observed or read simply as a text that shares no common voice to acknowledge this sacred exchange. Without this mutual sharing of proclamation and response in a rich variety of ritual languages, there is really nothing to say and the liturgy is mute.

Otto Semmelroth, the twentieth-century Jesuit sacramental theologian, spoke about the centrality of Christ in this interchange.[18] He is *Wort und Antwort*, both Word and also Answer; God's promise (Word) incarnate in him and Christ's willing surrender of himself in love (Answer) completes this redemptive dialogue. The complementarity of Word and Answer are embodied in ambo and table, and in the liturgy the assembly hears the promise, responds in faith, and asks to be held by him and to hold him as he offers his praise and thanks back to the Father. Christ's saving deeds are now inseparable from the Body's own loving surrender. In the cadence of eucharistic praying, to name God and praise God's holy name becomes a revelatory moment of God's life in our midst, the cause of our joy, our hope in sorrow, our life amid impending death, love resonant in everything. As the Exsultet proclaims and the Church sings, "Let this building shake with joy, / Filled with the mighty voices of the people." The holy dwelling "shakes" and grace is there in plenitude when the sacramental Body proclaims and responds in invocation and evocation.

(2) *The voice of the Body in the communal reading of sacred texts*—Christ is speaking "when the holy scriptures are read in the Church" (SC 7) and this locutionary presence is itself a rich matrix of symbolic relationships. First, there is the scriptural canon, from which the lectionary passages are taken. What is proclaimed and heard in these texts takes the form of communal sacred speech expressed in narrative and song, poetry and personal testimony, lament and brokenness, the offshoot of both guilelessness and of culpable infidelity. The stories testify

to a covenantal relationship with God that is both communal and individual, and is God's faithful response in mercy never to abandon the people. Such promises are not only written on "tablets of stone" (Exod 31:18) but etched upon the heart (Ezek 36:26); they are imaged in a parting sea, a pillar of fire (Exod 13:18, 22), and a rainbow in the sky (Gen 9:13), to name a few. This is the word that resonates throughout the Scriptures and its many faceted aspects of invocation and evocation: "For you are a people holy to the LORD your God; it is you the LORD has chosen out of all the peoples of the earth to be his people, his treasured possession" (Deut 14:2).

Since these Holy Scriptures "are read in the church," the voice of the readers is the communal voice of the whole; the preaching of the Scriptures the voice of Christ,[19] in the person of the preacher *in persona ecclesiae* that "breaks open that Word" so as to locate that living and active word in the context of *lo cotidiano*. Such a holy exchange—when received as Christ's own acting in us—stirs hearts, draws the Body into communion with her Head and heart, and announces there a word of life to the Body as a Spirit-filled, embodied voice for the whole world. "Go in peace, glorifying the Lord by your lives" is the culminating *missio*. Sacred speech in the liturgy is never meant to be an in-house and private conversation, but a generative and life-giving word of "grace, reconciliation, and eternal life: Jesus Christ," to echo Rahner's powerful claim for God's saving acts in Jesus.[20]

It is for this reason that the lectionary book has a revered place, the ambo, as its reading table and place of proclamation. It is a place of nourishment for the communion incarnate, of the "feast" as Lafont calls it, just as the table of Eucharist holds its bounty, "especially when it is addressed and exchanged in those moments of joy" that the liturgical feasting expresses.[21] The various authors and communities who shaped these texts are now part of that holy communion. The assembly's covenantal seal on the Body's event of speaking and hearing the word is expressed with ritual gestures and attitudes of attentive proclaiming and listening, chanted response, standing and bowing, the signing of the body, and the acclamation of praise: "Thanks be to God!" "Praise to you, Lord Jesus Christ!" Spoken words and actions together (voice and movement in harmony) communicate in one voice the saving deeds announced as word of God and the presence of Christ. They are *kerygmatic* (announcing the offer of grace) in a new key, so that in the event of proclamation they witness to the faith of our forebears and our own identity with this word, which is now our word, "fulfilled in [our] hearing" (Luke 4:21).

All that happens in the Liturgy of the Word, therefore, shares in a moment when the Body's voice participates in Christ's voice who is speaking, not only in the scriptural words themselves, but also "speaks volumes" through the ritual way the book is carried to and from the ambo from which it is proclaimed, in the sister and brother whose voice is our communal voice, and in the preacher who speaks not his own word but a saving word that wells up through the stirring of the Spirit. All of this helps and gives expression to the sacramental Body's voice in this redemptive dialogue. In this voice, she gives testimony to her reality as a "new people" and as a community of hearers of the word and "bearers of the same word in the Church and in the world, at least by the witness of their lives."[22]

(3) *The multidimensional body language of the Body: more than mere words*—As was noted above, spoken words and gestures together cooperate in the proclamatory event. The stress and accent of the voice participate in this symbolic exchange because they share in the particular poetic rhythm that characterizes revelatory speech.[23] What does this suggest concerning the proclamation of the word and how its celebration can be more living and active within the sacramental Body? In addition, how does the communal Body's voice and active listening and attentive presence allow the Holy Spirit to breathe that sustenance into the singular vessel so that, as the Lectionary for Mass asserts, "the word of God becomes the foundation of the liturgical celebration and the rule and support of all our life" (no. 9)? Indeed, the multidimensional communication acts that make up the ritual word, as the patterned mode of oral expression of the liturgy, especially in the proclamation of the Scriptures, is a privileged testimony to a life in communion, in our clinging to Christ and allowing him to cling to us.

It would seem important to note some aspects that raise this ritual voice and the word of God it announces to a level of attentive intentionality so that what she actually utters "sounds like a Body wedded to Christ" and, most importantly, makes room for this Christ "to be speaking when the holy scriptures are read in the Church." Simple modes of stress and accent in the ritual celebration make that poetic discourse more transparent on a variety of levels and dimensions, even though they may not be apparent to the Body on the everyday level of cognition alone.

We spoke briefly of the ambo and the book, and there is even deeper resonance attached to their actual crafting and use. Although the written text itself is not the proclamation and the ambo where it rests is not the sole place where the word of God is heard, as sacramental symbols within the liturgy they *are* the physical locus of the sacramental Body's proclaiming and hearing the word of God. The General Instruction of the Roman Missal highlights that the place of proclamation enhances the centrality of this oral event in the Body's self-expression. It simply says,

> The dignity of the Word of God requires that in the church there be a suitable place from which it may be proclaimed and toward which the attention of the faithful naturally turns during the Liturgy of the Word. (GIRM 309)

Sumptuous ornamentation in liturgical materials as an end in itself does not impart dignity. However, what is beautiful and treasured gains dignity in its intentional and caring use and in the identifying relationship it has to those who use it. From this perspective, in the context of *lo cotidiano*, employing the artistic vision and the work of the people's hands in fashioning the ambo and the books of prayer speaks in a clear voice about the honor and respect of the Body who worships there. Just as the adage says, "You are what you eat" (an appropriate metaphor for a eucharistic people), the sacramental Body is what she speaks, and how she speaks, which is affirmed in the importance placed on this speech act.

The rich devotional tradition of Christianity has always honored this artistic dimension of liturgical enactment. For example, there is "a dual interaction between functional structure and external form, its ornamentation," notes the medieval art historian Otto Pächt, specifically concerning the design and illustration of liturgical books and their "integral spiritual aspect," which convey "a living testimony to the intellectual content acting through them." Even illiterate worshipers "instinctively felt" that relationship between matter and form. Besides its objective character as a book (and the same would hold true for all liturgical vessels of devotion), these beautiful texts "had [their] own special meaning as witness to the promise of salvation," what he later calls a "luminous aura."[24] In liturgical terms we have been considering, this luminescence may be more appropriately called in this case *a sacramental resonance.*

An *ambo* that is lovingly crafted for the expressed purpose of enthroning this sacramental presence, along with a fitting and beautiful book that holds the revelatory word, are vehicles that carry the voice of this Body. They are not static and passive "things," but actors within a lively exchange of grace. The intentionality in creating them and reverently using them (or not) *says* something, and it speaks volumes concerning the role of this saving proclamation as constitutive of the unity of this Body.[25] As incidental and quotidian as such matters may seem, amplification that allows the assembly to hear with ease and appropriate lighting that gives a focus to the centrality of the place of proclamation also "speak" of the Body's voice and ears in announcing the good news. Such examples simply highlight the ambo as a place where the ministers of the word, servants of its message, can be seen and heard by all who are gathered. Its prominence says something about the Body's own voice: "This is where Christ speaks and we find our voice," it says. "In this Word we find our life."

At the same time, the *lectionary* or *Gospel book,* as a ritual vessel, should bear that same dignity, both in its outward appearance and in how it is carried, lifted up, kissed, and incensed. They deserve "exceptional signs of respect," twentieth-century Dominican theologian I. M. Dalmais says, for they acknowledge the respect due to this holy word, for "in them, too, Christ, the subsistent Word in whom all scriptures have their fulfillment, makes himself heard or known in some degree."[26]

In sum, care for the holy things used in the Liturgy of the Word and for the gestures and quality of voice the Body uses to express its unity in invocation and evocation are not peripheral to the communication event to which these ritual actions give voice. They invite the assembly to turn toward the ambo and expectantly engage those who enter its sacred space for the "living and active" grace these words announce, particularly when they are given a ritual voice in the midst of the Body. Every actor enters the communion. The lector or priest's voice is not, in the end, her or his own. When the reader approaches the ambo and engages the book, the Body coalesces; Christ is speaking and has entrusted that it be heard in the medium of *these* voices in *this* time and place. Every community will do this with a reverence consistent with the cultural realities of the Body and the structural configuration of the space in which all are gathered. In some places, the decorated Gospel book processes through the assembly and the community responds with a bow of respect; other traditions offer the book to the Body and invite members to reach out to touch it or kiss it. The book is then placed "in repose," just as the sacramental elements are reposed. These examples of reverent intentionality are embodied responses to the sacramental presence of Christ, who speaks and is heard in this holy meeting.

The body language in all this cannot be overexaggerated or undervalued. It must fit the particular assembly, and what it proclaims should "sound like" this diverse ecclesial assembly united with her Lord, a singular vessel of devotion, proclaiming the deeds of God to all generations with the particular stress and accent that fit her. The communal reading of sacred texts and the body language that goes into that symbolic interchange is a privileged moment of the voice of the faithful. In whatever time and place, the universality of the Church and revelatory word entrusted to her finds a timbre and resonance that mirrors God's saving deeds fulfilled in their hearing. In the end, the biblical and ritual texts do not sit isolated upon a page as in a library. The ambo and lectionary that cradle these Scriptures are servants of the voice given to this Body to announce God's saving deeds, revealed now as a fresh word in this convocation of the Body of Christ. A closer look at a focal partner in this exchange is the presider/preacher, to which we will now turn.

(4) *The presider's ecclesial voice in prayer and preaching: transparent and resonant*—The leader of the liturgical assembly has a focal sacramental role that "bodies forth Christ" within the *totus Christus*, as *Sacrosanctum Concilium* 7 reminds us.[27] In terms of the presider's personal voice on behalf of the gathered community, therefore, its character is always an ecclesial voice; the presider acts *in persona Christi* precisely because he acts *in persona ecclesiae*.[28] From this perspective, and of particular importance for a study of the sacramental Body, that specifically sacramental presence is always and necessarily relational, dialogical, and participative at its core, because the presider gathers the community into communion as the Body of Christ at prayer. It is out of that experience of being the "gatherer," of bringing the scattered limbs of the Body together in prayer and praise with one mind and heart and voice,

that the presider's speech acts have a privileged role in the singular vessel of devotion.

The presider qua presider, therefore, never speaks in his own name, although the temptation to forget who one is, or a lack of attentive intentionality of the true rhythm and harmony of the liturgy, often gives lie to this focal sacramental principle. Given the vulnerable task of giving voice to Christ and the assembly, to the Head and members in communion, a closer look at how the presider's voice "sounds like Christ" and resonates in the Body so that it sounds the strains of assembly's own gathered communion seems an important clarification. In keeping with the multidimensional aspects of this sacramental voice discussed above, we will look at the actual orality of prayer and praise but will consider as well how the body language of liturgical leadership speaks volumes.

It is truly a charism for the presider's voice to "sound like Christ" so that the sacramental Body experiences its cohesion precisely in the timbre and sound of the leader that gathers them. Two aspects may describe the characteristics of this gift given to gather and build up the Body: *transparency* and *resonance*. We recall those early disciples who follow John the Baptist's summons: "Behold, the Lamb of God" (John 1:36 NABRE). Their response to this voice is to enter into a redemptive dialogue with Jesus, who asks in turn what they are seeking. This spiritual conversation leads to a whole new journey and identity for them. Similarly, the people of God come to the liturgy as hungry seekers of a word of life that promises a new relationship with Christ the Head and a new way of being with one another and the world in which they dwell. The gatherer's voice names this matrix of symbolic relationships from the very moment of the Body's convening, for it is this ecclesial voice that welcomes them at the door and greets the assembly now gathered as the Church at prayer. The invitation to the gathering speaks in the very name of the triune God who invites and hosts and waits upon them.

The mystery of sacramentality reveals that the ecclesial voice now has a specific voice. The presider welcomes and renews them in their new relational identity and in this personal voice situates the members ritually into communion. "Let us pray" is a bold act of communal faith, but it is also a vulnerable risk to undertake. What if nothing prayerful seems to be happening, or the assembly seems scattered elsewhere, preoccupied by individual concerns rather than in the unity of the Body of which each is an essential sinew that holds them together in unity? The liturgical leader, in the midst of this vulnerability, sets the tone with voice and body language, to cooperate with the divine grace that is the source of this great in-gathering. By means of his bodiliness, the presider collects the Body in prayer and reminds each of his or her common place in the tent of mercy and the glory due God's name. Through this vehicle, he preaches the word with the authority of the shepherd and invites the Body to stand as one before the living God. What is perhaps most awesome here is that by means of this voice, the leader of the assembly addresses the divine One in their name. It is only then that the eucharistic gifts can be offered in union with Christ's own self-offering as a mutual exchange of gifts.

This is why the charism to gather the community "to sound like Christ" takes on a great and serious responsibility as a resonant and transparent way of presiding. To become an icon that opens a doorway to encounter the Beloved One for whom we hunger, and who also clings to us in a passionate love, has less to do with having more education or a perceived greater holiness or a sanctioned assurance that one has been called to serve the Body in this fundamental role and voice. Only a faith-filled surrender can turn a presider's voice from being that of a lone wolf to the familiar voice of the good Shepherd. This is where *kenotic transparency* becomes the first rule for the presider's voice as the Body's instrument.

Iconic leadership of prayer recognizes that such self-emptying opens a window into the Body's relationship with the Love that summons them. In recognizing the triune embrace in the invitation of the one who gathers, the Body coalesces, members are knit together with the Spirit as the Fashioner, and Christ's own life is the muscle and sinew and lifeblood. As was mentioned in the first chapter, such refashioning of the Body into a new reality shares Christ's own bodily surrender to his Father and to those to whom he is sent and with whom he casts his lot.[29] The members of the assembly, by means of a regular and faithful act of worshipful surrender, discover their truest personal identity in handing themselves over to this common Father, but also and necessarily to the sister and brother present, whose sacramental bond with them occurs in the holding and being held by Christ. What the presider says, and how he says it, and the body language of hospitable invitatory prayer communicates the voice of Christ who says, "Come and see" (John 1:39), the pastor of souls who pitches his tent among us (see John 1:14). Just as the tradition speaks of the communion table as both the sign of unity and the source of its bond,[30] and since everything in the liturgy *matters* and *forms*, then the presider's words and manner and bodily presence communicates this twofold grace of the liturgical gathering, especially in the celebration of the Eucharist. Experience and instinct affirm the theological claim that the "voice" of the presider in all its multidimensional aspects can draw the Body in, or it can create an impenetrable wall between the sanctuary and the nave. When speaking liturgically, the presider's voice has the capacity to speak the truth of that triune embrace or to widen a chasm that frustrates that communion incarnate. Both vulnerable possibilities take place through the embodiment of the one who leads the assembly in prayer. What tips the scales in drawing the Body in and together (a vertical, horizontal, and depth movement) is kenotic transparency that does not cling to power or status, but has the resonance of a broken and wounded Lord who, "though he was in the form of God, did not regard equality with God as something to be exploited" (Phil 2:6), and to whom and in whose holy name

> every knee should bend,
>> in heaven and on earth and under the earth,
> and every tongue confess
>> that Jesus Christ is Lord,
>> to the glory of God the Father. (Phil 2:10b–11)

A final point regarding the presider's ecclesial voice must include the seminal speech act of *preaching*. The restoration of the importance of preaching in the Vatican II renewal of the liturgy has placed a heightened awareness on a charism that is, for the preacher who really is attentive to what this sacred trust entails, a singularly vulnerable act.[31] On one level, it places the patrimony of the sacred tradition into the words and voice of a person who shares the human need of mercy and forgiveness, who "thirsts for God, for the living God" (Ps 42:2), yet who, at the same time, must hand him- or herself over as the instrument and mouthpiece of that saving message.

Yet, the tradition rightly affirms that the preacher's is an honorable voice as well, as Paul reminds us in 1 Timothy. He holds up those who "rule well" and exhorts that these elders be received with attentive receptivity, precisely and especially, when they "labor in preaching and teaching" (5:17). Laborers of the word give flesh and blood in word and image to the proclamation of faith, embodied and revealed in the Scriptures and handed down through the apostolic preaching that grounds the Church's faith. This is what we mean that a christic resonance is an essential characteristic of the unified voice of the whole Body, now given focal expression here in the voice and person of those who, in the name of the Church, enter the ambo, open the holy book, and begin to speak. As the Body's voice, they preach Christ himself, whose very presence stands squarely in the center of this symbolic exchange of the preaching event. The preacher's own transparency in allowing the scriptural word the freedom to flow through the life of the community in order to enter the poetic cadence of his or her own life and faith enables its grace-filled resonance to "sound like Christ" as Word and Answer in this great redemptive dialogue. The preached word helps to shape a *communitas verbi*, to whom his Son clings and who cling to him as one Body. "May the Lord be in my mind, on my lips, and in my heart," the preacher's silent prayer says, "that I may worthily and fittingly proclaim the holy Gospel."

Preaching, therefore, is a vulnerable but also a bold act of a voice that dares to speak on behalf of the Body of Christ in the Lord's name. "Is not my word like fire, says the LORD, and like a hammer that breaks a rock in pieces?" Jeremiah stubbornly reminds us (23:29). And yet the task of the preacher is also as a humble holder of the dear ones, as Isaiah tells us as well:

> The LORD GOD has given me
>   the tongue of a teacher,
> that I may know how to sustain
>   the weary with a word.
> Morning by morning he wakens—
>   wakens my ear
> to listen as those who are taught. (50:4)

Indeed, as Isaiah exclaims further on,

> How beautiful upon the mountains
>   are the feet of the messenger who announces peace,
> who brings good news,
>   who announces salvation,
>   who says to Zion, "Your God reigns." (52:7)

91

This is the vulnerable, kenotic, resonant transparency of the voice of the preacher who gathers the Body into communion.

The author of Hebrews knew this two-edged sword (Heb 4:12), and Paul acknowledges that true spiritual authority and power "is made perfect in weakness" so that "whenever I am weak, then I am strong" (2 Cor 12:9, 10). Such handing over of his life in such a public manner laid bare his kenotic vulnerability as one who proclaims Christ crucified when he says to the community at Corinth,

> For I decided to know nothing among you except Jesus Christ, and him crucified. And I came to you in weakness and fear and in much trembling. My speech and my proclamation were not with plausible words of wisdom, but with the demonstration of the Spirit and of power, so that your faith might rest not on human wisdom but on the power of God. (1 Cor 2:2–5)

This power is communicated through the vessel's resonant and transparent voice, that of an iconic preacher who opens a door into the mystery through the fashioning of real words in real time that bear the imprint of the Spirit's inscription. Any other "stress and accent" focused on self is that of a voice engaged in what can truly be called *idol* chatter, self-enclosed, shaped by one's own control issues or, dare we say it, by a laziness that simply satisfies itself with pious platitudes and surface reference to the texts. And yet, the sacramental Body invites so much more through the rhythm of the members' own search for holiness and the wrestling with the complexity of life today. Indeed—if the presider is attentive to it—the assembly participates in effecting the reality that sacramental peaching signifies, that is, a voice that sounds like Christ, that speaks volumes about the world, and that imagines a new reality, a new way of being together, and a unified voice that bears the message that consecrates everything.

The communal voice in one voice is personal and individual, but, at the same time, is the same voice that unites the entire celebration. It speaks for Christ, for the gathered Body, for the tradition, and for all far off who are invited by this voice and body language to enter and find the place where the Lover of souls dwells. As the United States Conference of Catholic Bishops' recent document reiterates,

We should also note that the preaching of a homily, since it occurs in the context of the Church's liturgy, is by definition a profound ecclesial act, one that should be in evident communion with the Church's Magisterium and with the consciousness that one stands in the midst of a community of faith....It is directed *from* faith, that of the Church and of the ordained minister who preaches in the name of Christ and his Church, *to* faith—that is, the faith of the Christian community gathered in a spirit of prayer and praise in the presence of the Risen Christ.[32]

So this voice *is* privileged, while at the same time it relies precisely on its willingness to descend into the "abyss of plenitude" in God's pierced heart[33] and becomes pierced like Christ, diving into the depths of the heart of the wounded, hungry, thirsty ones who gather to constitute the Church. The presider's voice, perhaps most transparently in the "hungry place" of the pulpit,[34] is always a conversation that envelops ambo and table, Word and Answer, and effects the reality it signifies, the sacramental Body proclaimed as the Body of Christ.

Fr. Josef Jungmann, eminent twentieth-century liturgical historian, emphasized this integral relationship, especially in his foundational work of making the Vatican II liturgical reform a reality in the years before and following the Council. He reminded us of the "mystagogical function" of preaching in the liturgy, which serves to provide "the link connecting God's Word as proclaiming the readings with the Eucharistic celebration." In this organic unity, "the homily is not an arbitrary interruption of the liturgy, but it is an integral and organic part of *'a fully developed act of worship.'*"[35] The presider speaks in a variety of ritual expressions from both ambo and altar, from the chair and in the midst of the Body gathered, with a voice that is integral and fully developed in its own right.

(5) *Active listening and silence as crucial in the dialogical voice of the Body*—Because the liturgy in its rhythm is relational, dialogical, and participative, what the mouth utters, in the name of Jesus, needs to be in harmony with the Head to which she clings and that clings to her. The revelatory Word of God comes forth from the mouth of God and is spoken *to* created reality, and so it is first heard and received through the Body's ear—an ear that listens, discerns, and knows this voice, as

opposed to "background noise" and foreign voices that dampen or mute the Spirit. The attitude is, as we have been saying, an active intentionality. This active listening itself provides spiritual nourishment for the Body and shapes a voice of resonance.

Jesus, beloved Word of the Father, speaks in the power of the Spirit that led him into the desert in Matthew's Gospel: "One does not live by bread alone, but by every word that comes from the mouth of God" (4:4). The nourishment of which he speaks requires a metaphorical "empty stomach" that allows the Spirit to enter into the singular vessel of devotion. As the spiritual writer Caryl Houselander has described so beautifully, Mary is the model of this vessel, for the poor and humble circumstances of her call hollow out a space and a voice within her to become the "Reed of God" that sings the song of liberation and salvation (Luke 1:46–55). This Mater Ecclesiae is a "willing table having space for the Bread of Life," as the Akathist Hymn sings of her. Her attentive emptiness, a true kenosis of body, mind, and spirit, is the prophetic way of the sacramental Body at prayer. As Houselander says, "It is emptiness like the hollow in the reed, the narrow riftless emptiness which can only have one destiny: to receive the piper's breath and to utter the song that is in his heart."[36] And so communal silence always accompanies listening, and the two in tandem are essential characteristics of the sacramental Body, if she is to hear a word that will rouse her (Isa 50:4) to be the Spirit-filled, resurrected Body of Christ that she is. Such pregnant emptiness reaches to every dimension of the Body's wholeness. The ineffable mystery of God's communication with humanity teaches that it is only when we have nothing to say that something can be received as a gift. Generative silence is the ground of expectancy. The prophet Zephaniah considers it a prerequisite to all gestures of praise and thanks and self-offering:

Be silent before the Lord GOD!
　For the day of the LORD is at hand;
the LORD has prepared a sacrifice,
　he has consecrated his guests. (1:7)

Sacrosanctum Concilium 30 expressed the importance of this silent character of the assembly in the celebration of the liturgy, when it states,

To promote active participation, the people should be encouraged to take part by means of acclamations, responses, psalmody, antiphons, and songs, as well as by actions, gestures, and bodily attitudes. And at the proper times all should observe a reverent silence.

Silence, then, is consonant with fully participative and conscious worship. However, this aspect has not been understood well since the liturgical reform of Vatican II, nor has it been implemented in a way that is in harmony with the participative activity of the liturgical assembly. Noting that this is "a general rule in liturgical functions," The *General Instruction for the Liturgy of the Hours* notes the importance of "The Sacred Silence," but is half-hearted in affirming its importance:

> The purpose of this silence is to allow the voice of the Holy Spirit to be heard more fully in our hearts, and to unite our personal prayer more closely with the word of God and the public voice of the Church. In introducing silence we must use prudence....Care should be taken that such a silence neither deforms the structure of the Office, nor upsets or bores the participants.

And yet, the General Instruction of the Roman Missal (2011) considers such silence to be an important part of the structure of liturgical rites. It is a natural rhythm that should be honored by the presider when he invites the assembly to be praying together as one Body. "Let us pray," the Instruction states, "and everybody, together with the Priest, observes a brief silence so that they may become aware of being in God's presence and may call to mind their intentions" (no. 54). Yet, little more is said about how this silence is a holistic, communal act that matters and forms the unity of the Body at prayer. The emphasis appears to emphasize a ritual obligation and an individual discipline of devotion, rather than a way of listening and hearing together that itself binds the scattered members of the assembly into a sacramental Body at prayer and a singular vessel of devotion. GIRM 45 notes,

> Sacred silence also, as part of the celebration, is to be observed at the designated times [SC 30]. Its nature, however, depends on the moment when it occurs in the different parts of the

SINGULAR VESSEL OF DEVOTION

celebration. For in the Penitential Act and again after the invitation to pray, individuals recollect themselves; whereas after a reading or after the Homily, all meditate briefly on what they have heard; then after Communion, they praise God in their hearts and pray to him.

Even before the celebration itself, it is a praiseworthy practice for silence to be observed in the church, in the sacristy, in the vesting room, and in adjacent areas, so that all may dispose themselves to carry out the sacred celebration in a devout and fitting manner.

The silence and listening of which we are speaking is of a different order and purpose. There needs to be a distinction between the two, as nuanced and subtle as it is. Sacred silence within the Body is neither, first and foremost, a ritual directive, nor a chance for an individual to enter into a personal reflection on her or his own sinfulness, nor an acknowledgment of one's need of God or awe in the divine presence, as rich as these practices could be.[37] Furthermore, it is not the passivity of a worshiping assembly that observes silently, perhaps following a text, while the ministers speak or act in their name. Generative communal silence has a different attentive intentionality. What is primary here is a gathered Body honoring silence together, responding to an invitation to enter its sacred confines as a unifying act, facilitated by leaders of prayer who speak in the name of Christ and Christ's Body. When the rhythm of the entire liturgy ebbs and flows with word and silence, song and gesture, a way of being the Body of Christ in union with her Lord deepens and conforms the Body in its holistic integrity. This requires an emptiness that becomes a spaciousness for the word of God and for the movement of the Spirit to "resound with joy," as the Exsultet announces.

In a wonderful short essay in his book *Words and Gestures in the Liturgy*, entitled "Being Silent," Italian presbyter Antonio Donghi notes that such silence is not the emptiness of "being forced to be silent." Rather, "being silent reveals particular attitudes that arise from an interior richness: the living consciousness of finding oneself in the presence of God who reveals his face and salvation to us....Silence allows the intensity of the human heart's pleading for God to come."[38] What is more, the silence is a mutual unfolding between God and the

96

Body that bears the name of his own Son, as the Wisdom of Solomon describes:

> For while gentle silence enveloped all things,
> and night in its swift course was now half gone,
> your all-powerful word leaped from heaven, from the royal
>   throne,
> into the midst of the land that was doomed. (18:14–15a)

Silence is the space of enfolding and the environment for the Spirit's hallowing, for Donghi insists, "God lives this silence, since God's interior vitality is silence....Silence is never empty, a useless time to be filled. Instead, it is the realm of divine abundance. It is the epiclesis of the believing soul that longs for the Absolute."[39]

If this is surely true of each of the individual members in the assembly, we can only imagine the power and grace that flows from a union of mind and heart and spirit by the community gathered as one Body and Spirit in Christ. Such "interior vitality" of which he speaks flows through the sinews and breathes the Spirit. This attitude is not a natural way of being and proceeding, especially in contemporary culture, but when it is nurtured and honored and consistent as a natural way that the assembly experiences itself precisely as a sacramental Body, the sacramental bond effects the reality it signifies with greater transparency and resonance. Standing, praying, kneeling, and sitting together in such richness speaks volumes, and it is palpably felt and intensified the more the ear is attentive to what may happen and how God may then reveal the divine love through word, song, gesture, and text that accompany it. It can only be grasped as a unified act by a participating and consciously active assembly by faithfully *doing and being this* in memory of him.[40]

Admittedly, such silent listening as a ritual communal practice takes time to shape and needs ministers of ritual and prayer who are comfortable with letting a community develop the ears and the empty spaciousness that is fashioned through handing herself over, week after week, as the Body of this generative Son of the Father's silent creation. Once again, just as the voice of the Body's tenor and resonance is centered in Christ, so is its silence as a dialogical voice in loving communication with its source and summit. Through this way of being together, Christ is acting in them and actually speaking in them, communicating in the Spirit the Father's embrace that often needs no words and cannot be spoken audibly without accompanying times that allow that embrace to speak silently. This is a poetic ambiguity whose grace and meaning can only be a revelatory activity of the Body, as we said, by "doing and being this in memory of Him." John of the Cross says it so simply, speaking to the individual soul, and his rich spiritual wisdom takes on a renewed meaning in this context of the singular vessel of devotion. John says, "The Father spoke one Word, which was his Son, and this Word he speaks is always in eternal silence, and in silence must be heard by the soul."[41]

A community slowly formed in the practice of communal silence begins to feed on its riches, which will radiate out into every aspect of the shared celebration of the Body and its internal communion as members united to their Head, who clings to them and they to him. The ascetical tradition has known this as a spiritual practice for contemplatives.[42] Shared silence is the gift of this tradition to the entire Christian community, whose focal act of prayer is the liturgy of the Church. In that light, the Syrian monk St. Isaac of Nineveh's instruction in the seventh century still speaks volumes to our time and the liturgy's bonding. As he says,

> Silence like the sunlight will illuminate you in God and will deliver you from phantoms of ignorance. Silence will unite you to God himself….In the beginning we have to force ourselves to be silent. But then there is born something that draws us to silence. May God give you an experience of this "something" that is born of silence.[43]

Since all members and movements of the sacramental Body act in relational harmony, active listening and silence are not ends in themselves. The integral transformation that happens in the liturgical assembly at prayer—what Isaac calls this "something"—is to prepare a consecrated people, who hand on that gift for the life of the world. Thomas Merton emphasized the apostolic telos of silence as a gift to the world, one that "teaches Christ" and "the silence of the Resurrection." In this sense,

> Silence is ordered to the ultimate summing up in words of all we have lived for. We receive Christ by hearing in the word

of faith. We work out our salvation in silence and hope, but sooner or later comes the time when we must confess Him openly before men [and women], then before all the inhabitants of heaven and earth…silence is ordered to that final utterance. It is not an end in itself."[44]

The generativity of silence to shape apostolic mission has St. Paul's own conversion as a model and inspiration, passed on to us in his own conversion account in the Letter to Galatians. His story of a radically new self-identity in Christ for mission is not a description of being knocked off a horse by a bolt of lightning (Acts 9:1–9). In Paul's own account, the need for the reflective spaciousness required to receive the summons that will orient his whole life and meaning is revealed as the fruit of an organic, embracing fruit of silence:

> But when God, who had set me apart before I was born and called me through his grace, was pleased to reveal his Son to me so that I might proclaim him among the Gentiles, I did not confer with any human being, nor did I go up to Jerusalem to those who were already apostles before me, but I went away at once to Arabia, and afterwards I returned to Damascus.
>   Then after three years I did go up to Jerusalem…. (Gal 1:15–18a)

This is a sacramental vessel and voice that is in harmony with the voice of the depths, who knows the desert emptiness and silence and the exercise of active listening. In this revelatory spiritual journey, Christ's face is revealed to Paul. He patiently absorbs it, learns at the feet of the apostles, and only then can preach and proclaim. This is the model of fruitful silence that is eminently participative and communal within the liturgy and needs the patient discipline of sustained practice so that the ear can hear, the voice can speak, and the silence that is born there shares the "interior vitality" of God, who is always and forever speaking within this communion of love we invoke "in the name of the Father, and of the Son, and of the Holy Spirit."

(6) *The particular richness of music and singing as a proclamation of the Body's "communion incarnate"*—The final point of discussion regarding

the quality of transparent resonance in the voice and ear of the sacramental Body highlights the particular sonority that music and singing bring to the unity of the assembly at prayer. Congregational singing and shared listening uniquely gather a disparate gathering into one voice, whose activity sounds like Someone and does something (circulates grace) that speaks to the unity of the whole Body. As A. G. Martimort says,

> Song is also regarded as a means of manifesting a unanimity of outlook, because by its rhythm and melody it produces such a fusion of voices that there seems to be but a single singer. As a matter of fact, once there is a question of more than a small group of people, song alone makes it possible for an assembly to express itself as one.[45]

This fusion happens on many levels and it is a gratuitous gift given even before it is received in the enactment. The 2007 document entitled *Sing to the Lord: Music in Divine Worship* highlights the vertical, horizontal, and depth dimensions of this in-gathering that music accomplishes in a way unique to its mode of expression. As the bishops say in its opening paragraphs,

> (1) God has bestowed upon his people the gift of song. God dwells within each human person, in the place where music takes its source. Indeed, God, the giver of song, is present whenever his people sing his praises.
>
> (2) A cry from deep within our being, music is a way for God to lead us to the realm of higher things. As St. Augustine says, "Singing is for the one who loves." Music is therefore a sign of God's love for us and of our love for him. In this sense, it is very personal. But unless music sounds, it is not music, and whenever it sounds, it is accessible to others. By its very nature song has both an individual and a communal dimension. Thus, it is no wonder that singing together in church expresses so well the sacramental presence of God to his people.[46]

As a constituent element of the voice and ear of the sacramental Body, therefore, singing as a gift from the Giver of all gifts finds its incarnate home in the gathered assembly at prayer and is a privileged expression of the God who speaks and truly sings within the Body that is united as members to its Head, who clings to his Body and they to him. As the document insists, "Indeed, God, the giver of song, is present whenever his people sing his praises." Christ is incarnate Word that is the voice of this Body, it goes on to say, for it expresses a unique matter and form of this "sacramental presence." Thus, singing is essential to her sacramental self-expression and an essential dimension of the integrity of the praying Body of Christ.

As a sacramental activity, the eventful act of liturgical singing is not first ornamentation or background music or something to fill in the gaps or bridge different parts of the whole celebration. However, the way the liturgical assembly often employs music, both choral and instrumental, has often treated the sacramental act of singing in a perfunctory fashion. We choose music for different parts of the liturgy and for different cultural expressions that make up the assembly, and then we add congregational responses to the proper parts of the Mass, yet something of the mystery dimension with which music cooperates is often left as an untapped resource. Yet, what if Martimort's bold contention that "song alone makes it possible for an assembly to express itself as one" is true? How might that change the attentive intentionality a community and its leaders give to the particular richness of music and singing as a proclamation of the Body's "communion incarnate?" How does it participate in the poetic richness of the sacramental Body's presence and action as a singular vessel of devotion? This area of music and liturgy deserves greater appreciation, and the work of composers and musicians who serve the assembly in this fashion would need to have their rightful place in the central discussions preparing a local Church's common celebration of the sacred mysteries. As chapter 6 of *Sacrosanctum Concilium* set out as the Church began the current reform,

> The musical tradition of the universal Church is a treasure of inestimable value, greater even than that of any other art. The main reason for this pre-eminence is that, as sacred song united to the words, it forms a necessary or integral part of the solemn liturgy.
>
> Holy Scripture, indeed, has bestowed praise upon sacred song, and the same may be said of the fathers of the Church and of the Roman pontiffs....

> Therefore sacred music is to be considered the more
> holy in proportion as it is more closely connected with the
> liturgical action, whether it adds delight to prayer, fosters
> unity of minds, or confers greater solemnity upon the sacred
> rites. (no. 112)

To advance the point, further, though, singing and musical expression
are not only "a necessary or integral part of the solemn liturgy." We
can assert that they act from the inside out to transform the assembly itself as a transparent and resonant sacramental Body, and that its
sounding penetrates deeper than a "unity of minds" to actually shape
the organic integrity of the Body through its enactment. From this perspective, the singing assembly's integral ritual relationship to what she
celebrates is made manifest. Without singing, her true communal voice
is muted and silenced in ways that can never be captured using spoken
words alone. Singing together as a partner in her body language, resonates "as a cry deep within her being," to use the bishops' images, and
announces a new reality. This realm, where such cries and longing and
joys are heard in a new voice, is where, the Scripture says, "every crea-
ture in heaven and on earth and under the earth and in the sea, and
all that is in them [is] singing..." (Rev 5:13a). The assembly's sonorous
chorus is a proclamation of a new song that participates in the reality
that it signifies. And "whenever it sounds," as *Sing to the Lord 2* says, it
resonates a melodic harmony that reaches beyond the sanctuary to all
time and place and nations to communicate the truth of the prophesy
of all things fulfilled and completed in Christ. Its sacramentality bodies
forth Christ, who has made, through his own Body, a home "among
mortals," as "the Alpha and the Omega, the beginning and the end"
(Rev 21:3, 6) of all that is and all that will be. Revelation's song of all
creation sings,

> "To the one seated on the throne and to the Lamb
> be blessing and honor and glory and might
> forever and ever!"
> And the four living creatures said, "Amen!" And the
> elders fell down and worshiped. (Rev 5:13b–14)

Something greater than a song unto itself is at work here. The
choral dimensions are cosmic, rich in theological meaning, spiritual

depth, and evangelical reach. Worshiping assemblies that respect the unique medium of music and song have a felt knowledge of how such praying gathers and fuses the poetic richness of the sacramental Body's presence and action as a singular vessel of devotion. It is a particular vehicle of sacramental grace. The instrumentality of the Body's choral voice deepens the bond with Christ, one another, and with all that lives and breathes to praise the Lord with "a new song, his praise in the assembly of the faithful" (Ps 149:1; 150:6). In short, liturgical singing has a singularly powerful role in the proleptic anticipation of the eschatological fullness for which all creation longs. Through the lens of an attentive liturgical spirituality, musical expertise is not the primary factor here, but simply a willing communal voice to sing God's praise. How local liturgical leaders, composers, and musicians give shape and place to that awesome act of the Body's praise and thanks is a gift they give to the gift of Christ's Body they have been called to serve and nurture and gather as a community into communion.

As we make music and listen to its sound within the gathered Body in what we have called *communion incarnate*, "we enter into harmony with each other, our deeper selves, and Christ, and are enriched," as contemporary theologian and musician Maeve Heaney, VDMF, has noted in *Music as Theology: What Music Says about the Word.*[47] This is why we say that there is a *particular richness* to this aspect of the sacramental Body's voice. It employs what Heaney describes elsewhere as "the aesthetic patterns within which we try to express, make (*poesis*), and externalize in a new and creative way something that we have known, felt, tasted, and experienced" and to do this "in a receptive mode, through the sense, *before* we try to comprehend or explain it."[48]

Sing to the Lord 124 emphasizes, with perhaps a bit of dualism, that this dimension of the sacramental Body's voice must be honored and embraced. It says, "Music does what words alone cannot do. It can express *a dimension of meaning and feeling* that words alone cannot convey. While this dimension of an individual musical composition is often *difficult to describe*, its *affective power* should be carefully considered along with its textual component."[49] Such intentional attentiveness to all of this illustrates profoundly Ghislain Lafont's reverence for the voice that speaks within the Body at worship, whose words at the outset of this chapter provided an imaginative foundation to it. "Discourse is," he says, "first of all, voice; it is song; it is music."[50] The poetic richness of this "matrix of symbolic relationships" in which music and song lend their voices gives a profound and transparent resonance to the voice *doing this* and *being this* in memory of him.

Who is speaking within and for the Body matters and forms—One final caveat must serve as a necessary epilogue to this discussion of the resonance of sacred speech in the sacramental Body. The sound and body language that make up the Body, and of those that speak in privileged voices at times *in persona Christi* and *in persona ecclesiae*, must include and embrace diverse voices. What is more, the actual aural experience of such voices heard in their rich and mellifluous sonority gives full and true character to the singular vessel's vertical, horizontal, and depth dimensions.

The ramifications of this challenge are simple, but they also carry a host of unconscious dynamics at work in an ecclesial Body that is universal and particular, inclusive and yet clearly defining in its structural unity. Cultural and institutional traditions and roles also affect the complexity of its implementation in a myriad of conscious and unconscious ways. However, from the perspective of this theological and spiritual discussion, a convincing case can be made that speaking and hearing women's and men's voices—together and in antiphonal mutuality—changes the tenor of the sound the Body makes. In addition, young people, emerging adults, faithful middle-aged members, and elder wisdom voices can speak together with a harmony and a texture that a restricted, communal voice that is overwhelmingly male, ordained, professional, or taken over by those who have staked out the ambo or the interceding prayer as their private preserve can never hope to do. The sacramental Body of Christ needs to "sound like she truly is" so that the transparency and resonance of the assembly's voice can resound her praise and lament and joy in a manner that evokes the one Body to respond "with one heart and mind and voice."

This is not to denigrate legitimate roles of sanctioned and sacramental leadership and service. Unity in a plurality that respects the local Church's journey toward wholeness and transformation, however, may require different approaches than current practice embodies. Yet, an attentive intentionality to the sacramental Body's voice offers so much more than our previous attempts at a unified liturgical community have shown. At the least, it should be a matter of a free, earnest, and respectful conversation within the Body of Christ, listening to all the diverse perspectives that go into making her the gift she is for the life of the world. Given that, the theological and liturgical vision set out here suggests that when communities honor the richness and take the risk to make this diversity an integral and rhythmic character to her everyday speech acts and body language, *something happens* that cooperates with the Spirit's fashioning of an integral, healthy, vibrant Body of Christ. As was mentioned, *who* is speaking within and for the Body *matters* and *forms* the wondrous complexity of limbs and sinews, and the sounds and actions, of an assembly that truly is communion incarnate, the *totus Christus* in real flesh, who speaks as one voice of God's saving acts in Jesus. Genesis keeps calling us to this.

> So God created humankind in his image,
>   in the image of God he created them;
>   male and female he created them. (Gen 1:27)

And St. Paul gives even richer contours to that unity when he says, "For all of you are one in Christ Jesus. And if you belong to Christ, then you are Abraham's offspring, heirs according to the promise" (Gal 3:28b–29).

Karl Rahner spoke at the dawn of the Second Vatican Council of "God's self-disclosure in word"[51] as a moment of grace that is taking place anew in every age and people. Such an intimate understanding of the incarnation suggests that once this Word enters into the world, God is forever exposed and vulnerable, as if to say, "Here is who I AM." And this means that those who are God's living testimony in mind and heart and body and spirit bear the christic marks of that rich trust the divine One has placed in the Body of Christ, hearers of the word and bearers of its life and meaning for us and for all creation. The Lord's summons to Ezekiel is our own: "Mortal, all my words that I shall speak to you receive in your heart and hear with your ears" (Ezek 3:10b). It is out of that receptive willingness to hear that the voice can speak with sacramental integrity.

To engage the truth of the voice is a risk. Our communion incarnate can, through its voice and body language, mute this Word, dismiss it, even labor to destroy its efficacy and its unanimity. On the other hand, and this is the greater promise, the sacramental Body can hand herself over, and risk to listen to the Spirit's subtle voice always speaking a fresh Word in every age. Such a charismatic voice and stirring always calls the Body home to her dwelling "through him, and with him, and in him." Such a homecoming in every dimension discovers there her true identity and source, Christ Jesus, the Father's Word of grace, in whom she lives and moves and has her being (Acts 17:28). From that heart she speaks the offer of redemptive mercy and grace to all who have ears to hear. Acknowledging the role of the communal voice within this hallowed habitation, we now move to a consideration of the environment and space in which the Body dwells, what we will call the sacred space as a house of prayer for the Body, as a final dimension of this singular vessel of devotion.

Chapter 4

A Space that Has a Name and a Face

The Environment in Which the Body Dwells

The first step in the creation of an environment for worship is therefore the sanctification of the hearts of worshipers or, rather, the realization of the holiness already there. This realization is achieved as they turn from self to God present in the faith of the community.

That is why we have always to remember that holiness is not fundamentally a moral quality. It is rather a unique experience of Presence.

John Main, *The Christian Mysteries: Prayer and Sacrament*[1]

SACRED SPACES FOR WORSHIP are not passive entities. They provide a resonant, focal environment for the gathering of the baptized to constitute the Church, where Christ is present in four distinct but inseparable modes, as *Sacrosanctum Concilium* 7 has articulated. In harmony with the liturgical ritual and those who pray and sing within her walls, sacred space is dynamic, relational, and participative; it receives the assembly and offers a gift in return. When these mutual

107

dimensions of sacramental presence unfolding in Word and Sacrament take place within the liturgical space and its unique gifts are respected and engaged with an attentive intentionality, we can say that the praying Body as a singular vessel of devotion truly has a home, a hallowed place within the universal household of God. The spatial aspect of this sacramental exchange of gifts is the focus of this chapter, building upon the previous discussion of the movement and the voice of the singular vessel of devotion that gathers within her walls.

In particular, three aspects of this dynamism will help to clarify the importance of liturgical space as a "vigorously active" participant in a sacramental Body's living faith expressed in her prayer.[2] First, we will explore the relationship between a church building as a house of prayer and the Body who "lives" there. In particular, five sites of focal presence bodied forth in this encounter will be shown to galvanize the unity of the community as the *totus Christus*, clinging to Christ the Head who is inseparable from the members. Second, and much more briefly, the identity-making responsibility on the part of the assembly to do the "work" of making a sacred space her own demands an attentive intentionality that reverences and harmonizes with every aspect of liturgical praying. And *third*, leading to the concluding epilogue, the interaction of space, movement, and voice together coalesce to tap into the heart of the trinitarian communion that is her source and wellspring. From this vibrant center, as Louis Marie Chauvet has noted, the sacred space takes on the dynamism of a "symbolic space" that is unique, allowing the assembly to be taken "out of what is immediately useful, to create a space of *gratuitousness*."[3] The place in which the sacramental Body prays is, therefore, eucharistic. The physical space in which this flow of grace flourishes deserves our attention.

(1) *The relationship between a church building as a house of prayer and the Body who "lives" there: five sites of focal presence*—A body always inhabits a space. It is the "here and now" place of her beholding and symbolic communication among herself, others, and the world in which she dwells—all in a human journey seeking ultimate meaning. As a living body, she moves within this space and her voice speaks and is heard within the resonance of its environment. That is, at least, the hope when embodied humanity is seeking an integral life.

To realize this hope, the body intentionally and consciously places herself within a concrete "here and now" place, or she will not be wholly present *to*, *with*, or *for* the dynamic environment in which she relates. Hence, we often hear the term for a distracted or emotionally distant person that she or he is "not here" or "somewhere else." What is more, in this mutual exchange, the inhabited space can be a "safe space" or it can be hostile to her presence. Such aspects of mutual hospitality, when seen through the image and lens of the sacramental Body, take on theological importance and suggest liturgical consequences. In terms of the physical place of divine encounter, the theological relationship between the Body and the space of her sacramental encounter is crucial. The scattered parts of the Body are assembled here from the four winds[4] to realize the new life promised in baptism, for in this place she gives embodied expression to the desire and claim to be "clothed" in Christ (Gal 3:27) and to "have the mind of Christ" (1 Cor 2:16). As dwellers in the household of God, the sacramental Body inhabits this space as a "communion incarnate," a true and mystical presence with Christ the Head and with the members that are joined to him. Within the confines of this designated sacred space, as the Easter Exsultet proclaims, her communal voice shakes the building with her praise and thanks for God's saving acts in Jesus.[5]

Such a prayerful habitation consecrates the passing over from what is designed with great intentionality to be *sacred* to what is fashioned through sacramental practice to be *holy*. "Sacred," we could say, is the intended design for the *matter*, while what happens when the building is baptized and chrismated in the dedication (its lived *form*) constitutes what is "holy," consecrated, and set apart as a focal place of sacramental identity.[6] The divine is revelatory, at work within this relational whole. As Albert Rouet says, concerning the importance in the Hebrew Scriptures of the historicity of a place and the meeting that occurs there,

> Space becomes the site for a journey on which encounters take place where God takes the initiative to establish a personal and historical covenant. The *space* becomes an *event*, that is, a manifestation of God. We can say that sacred space in a biblical sense is *epiphany-like*...(and) this epiphany-like character includes a theology, that is, an explanation about God.[7]

What happens in this epiphanic liturgical space concerns the dynamic, relational, and participative activity of dwelling within the Body of Christ *as* the Body of Christ. In this lived holy space with Christ, the site for the epiphanic journey hosts this event that makes "really present" the deepest communion that transcends all places built by human hands alone. God takes the initiative and constructs a house of prayer for the Body who will live there. However, this is no magic intervention from beyond. The hard work of preparing liturgical environments cooperates with the divine initiative through gifted skill and theological wisdom incarnate in the crafters, in conversation with the people of God, and shaped through images and expectations borne of faithful practice. The envisioned place of worship becomes the chosen site, using the work of human hands, gracefully melding the interior journey with an exterior form that, through lived encounter with it, is recognized over time as resonant with holiness. As Paul tells the Athenians,

> The God who made the world and everything in it, he who is Lord of heaven and earth, does not live in shrines made by human hands, nor is he served by human hands, as though he needed anything, since he himself gives to all mortals life and breath and all things. From one ancestor he made all nations to inhabit the whole earth, and he allotted the times of their existence and the boundaries of the places where they would live, so that they would search for God and perhaps grope for him and find him—though indeed he is not far from each one of us. For "In him we live and move and have our being." (Acts 17:24–28a)

The holy place is an iconic testimony, a stopping place for refreshment on this journey to our true dwelling place where that intimacy of Head and members will share life eternal.

Considering this seminal manifestation of the new Jerusalem leads us back again to mine the richness of that chance meeting of the first disciples with Jesus in John 1, where they encounter this Lamb of God through John the Baptist's testimony and subsequent invitation, "Look, here is the Lamb of God." They respond by following Jesus, involving a pilgrimage of sorts to a place that is also a fulfillment of a desire:

> When Jesus turned and saw them following, he said to them, "What are you looking for?" They said to him, "Rabbi" (which translated means Teacher), "where are you staying?" He said to them, "Come and see." They came and saw where he was staying, and they remained with him that day. It was about four o'clock in the afternoon. (John 1:38–39)

The place where Jesus stays, in the spiritual abundance of this passage, is not first and foremost a hut of clay or stone. It is a place of active beholding and encounter, a "spiritual dwelling." Contemporary theologian of aesthetics Bert Daelemans, SJ, has even "baptized" the architectural space of the worshiping assembly as *synaesthetic, kerygmatic, and Eucharistic space* that, he claims in his book *Spiritus Loci: A Theological Method for Contemporary Architecture* (2015), is revelatory of an "itinerary that only ends in the Mystery with a Name and a Face." Indeed, the architectural space of a church is part of the embodied expression, he says, that hosts the formative journey that communal worship embraces, which is "to approach, enter, and appropriate the Mystery with a Name and a Face. Churches are places of encounter." Hence, he calls this dwelling "a Mystagogic space."[8] Liturgical space offers itself up as a place that participates in leading the assembly to its true home in the heart of God, in whom she lives and moves and has her being.

Indeed, the place and those who inhabit it for this graced encounter are, from the perspective of our exploration, "distinct but not separate," as the sacramental dictum insists. They are "in relationship." In the passage from John, the disciples saw the place where Jesus lives, but the quality of the encounter that occurs within this meeting place is what draws them in, and so they "remained with him that day." In that light, Daelemans suggests that when the worshiping assembly and the space in which they dwell are in rhythm and harmony, there is what we could describe here as a mutually enriching synergy taking place, where liturgical assemblies "can appropriate their churches, playing along with them as with a musical instrument, in order for them to sing."[9] Such imagery demonstrates the living faith that communicates through wood and stone and glass to help construct the singular vessel of devotion. As Daelemans says further, "Church building and liturgical rites belong together. The mystagogic meaning of a church comes to the fore when liturgically performed by a worshiping community. Hence, *mystagogic* space is meant to be *Eucharistic* space."[10]

At the beginning of this chapter, the Benedictine John Main exhorts about the priority of an interior holiness in the Body as a first step in imagining and creating an "environment for worship," which underlies the importance of the relationship between the house of prayer and the Body who finds communion within it. The space, to reiterate again, forms and it matters; it engages in communal soul making. For it is within this *mystagogic* and *eucharistic* space that the sacramental Body truly encounters and celebrates its identity as one whose mind and heart, whose movement and limbs, and whose resounding voice "cling to Christ and Christ to her." The place of worship, in relationship with a praying community, together shape a "symbolic space," as Chauvet notes, a "space of gratuitousness." Coming together in this chosen place of gathering together, there is—in truth—a marriage of heaven and earth. Pure gift, awesome meeting, and faith-filled hopes and desires find an epiphanic home. Jacob's experience on his journey, we could assert, continues in our own time: "Surely the LORD is in the place—and I did not know it....How awesome is this place! This is none other than the house of God, and this is the gate of heaven" (Gen 28:16–17).

The environment that now has a name and a face not only "sings"; it also embraces the gathered assembly as the *ekklesia*, the convoked and summoned people of God. A liturgical space constructed to be a sacred edifice wraps itself around the ritual Body to hold her as she encounters the awesome Mystery taking place, recognized now as consecrated and holy. The building serves the prayerful flourishing of the Body, and so is "distinct and yet never separate" from the wellspring flowing from the heart of Christ as the pulse of its living faith. Without this place of meeting, no space for Christian worship is holy. However, the sacramental exchange is mutual. Devoid of the sacramental Body and her rites, a beautiful design risks opting for a criterion of beauty that is appreciated only at face value (to play with the image) but has no unifying identity, no covenantal bond, no response in love back to the Giver of all gifts. It has no "name." It is through this dialogue between environment and those who worship that a liturgical space is consecrated by the holiness present in this encounter. The "intentional and significant"[11] ambiguity of the Church as an ecclesial body of faith, and the physical church as the architectural "skin" embracing the faithful as the Body of Christ, coalesce within this place and time to activate the grace of God's initiative to bring together the inside and the outside into a sacramental whole. As John Main says,

> The sacredness of the Church is nothing other than the holiness of the people who constitute the Church in any one time and in any one place. People in their kairos and topos, their time and space, are the chosen and dedicated of God. And so all consideration of the environment for worship must spring from this quintessential insight, that the environment for worship is a pure heart, because the holiness of a place is the holiness of the persons gathered there.[12]

In that understanding of the synergy of place and people and purposeful action, we will now look at five sites within the liturgical space itself that allow the sacramental Body to be and become herself in a particular time and place, an announcement of the taste of the promise and the kingdom toward which her pilgrimage as a Body tends. The five environmental sites of the *altar, ambo, baptismal font,* the *place of the presider,* and the *arrangement of the worshipers*—each placed in a harmonic relationship to the others—provide the setting for the sacred mysteries to be celebrated "in spirit and in truth" (John 4:23).

(a) The *altar* or table of the Eucharist has always functioned as a focal center of attention in Christian churches. Reverencing the role of those who gather around this focus, the mutual relationship between the table of the Lord and those who celebrate finds greater clarity.[13] Theologians Richard Vosko and Mark Wedig, OP, commenting on the General Instruction of the Roman Missal, illuminate the multivalent role the altar plays in eucharistic praying. They highlight "three complementary metaphors of the altar: altar, table, and center of thanksgiving" that help shape the wholeness of the liturgy that takes place in a house of worship. Commenting on GIRM 296–308, in dialogue with contemporary theologians and the rite of dedication itself, they explore the tensive role of sacrificial self-offering in union with Christ, the memorial meal that seals the covenantal bond, and the trajectory of eschatological fullness of which eucharistic communion is a taste of the promise to come:

113

A purposeful tension among these three gives a sense of the altar as a metaphor for the Church in adoration and thanksgiving before the Lord's own self-sacrifice on the Cross and the Church supping upon the food hosted by the Lord's bountiful love. Two meanings (altar and table) are communicated as God's gift to the people in Christ, emphasizing the Christological significance of all activity associated with the altar. What is clarified and underlined here in *GIRM 2002* is the third meaning of the altar, where the local assembly in union with the whole Church offers thanksgiving.[14]

This third meaning completes the mutual exchange of gifts inherent in any sacramental activity. To highlight the ecclesial communion signified by this threefold meaning of the altar, the authors note that GIRM 299 goes on to speak about the placement of this multivalent center of attention:

> 299. The altar should be built apart from the wall, in such a way that it is possible to walk around it easily and that Mass can be celebrated at it facing the people, which is desirable whenever possible. The altar should, moreover, be placed so as to be truly the center toward which the attention of the whole congregation of the faithful naturally turns. The altar is fixed and is dedicated.

Wedig and Vosko comment on the ecclesiological enactment such a placement offers, "so that the altar anchors both the assembly's worship and its adoration." All three aspects of sacrifice, meal, and adoration are part of the assembly's identity and devotion and not simply that of the presider and official ministers. Indeed, as they say further, citing *Sacrosanctum Concilium* 48, "the altar provides a way for the local Church *to identify itself* gathered around that altar in the act of offering as the Body of Christ itself" and clarifies that the constructed space and the altar placement are a symbolic expression of "the post-resurrection Church gathered in the Lord's presence."[15]

If the placement of the altar is to become a holy place, it is because of what the sacramental Body enacts there. The place of eucharistic offering, the document states, is a freely standing place, accessible, and draws the assembly toward it, "placed so as to be truly the center" of communal focus. This requires attentive intentionality. When such a consideration is not paramount, one can imagine spaces where the altar is perceived as a sacerdotal domain alone (a clerical sanctuary of sorts) and a place where something done by others is consecrated and, only then, the bounty of its boundaries leave the place and mingle with the faithful. However, St. Augustine's often-quoted dictum suggests a fuller reality and truth:

> If you, therefore, are Christ's body and members, it is your own mystery that is placed on the Lord's table! It is your own mystery that you are receiving! You are saying "Amen" to what you are: your response is a personal signature, affirming your faith. When you hear "The body of Christ," you reply "Amen." Be a member of Christ's body, then, so that your "Amen" may ring true! (Sermon 272)

If this awesome mystery is true, and the table of Eucharist the place of the Body's own visitation, then the altar—focal, easily accessible, and visible from all sides—should be clear and unequivocal. The altar where eucharistic praying around which the sacramental Body is gathered and summoned to *do* and therefore to *be*, "in memory of Him," speaks of this centrality, rather than of a place whose visible distance or one-sided placement suggests something merely done *for* them. In contrast, the gift-giving and thanksgiving from a disconnected altar, as valid and efficacious as it may be, mutes the mystery. Without a great effort at interior translation, such distancing can make the singular vessel's self-offering incidental, rather than assisting a communion of mind and heart where the members of the sacramental Body see their integral participation in the sacrifice, the meal, and the adoration as their own sacramental "right and duty, by reason of their baptism" (SC 14).

The placement of the altar often varies according to restrictions of existing space, a community's cultural memory, and catechesis. However, the impelling theological and pastoral need to consider the altar as always and necessarily in relationship to the primary celebrant of the liturgy—the Body of Christ in communion with her leaders and the universal Church—needs creative attention and priority. In contrast, when this relationship expressed in the altar's placement is devalued or even ignored in lieu of other considerations of perceived beauty, comfortable familiarity ("as we have known it"), or even the acknowledged

intransigence of existing dimensions and shapes, the relationship
between a church building and a house of prayer for a Body who
"lives" there is diminished. When altar and assembly are so distinct
and separate, it requires interior work to imagine what is in dynamic
harmony with the sacramental intention and what, in reality, obscures
it—all good intentions notwithstanding.[16] Authors such as Bouyer and
Martimort at the time of the Council, and contemporaries considered
here like Daelemans, Vosko and Wedig, Rambusch, and a host of other
liturgical theologians considering space provide creative and innova-
tive ways to make the altar "truly the center," a partner in bringing
about, as GIRM 294 insists,

> a close and coherent unity that is clearly expressive of the
> unity of the entire holy people. Indeed, the character and
> beauty of the place and all its furnishings should foster devo-
> tion and show forth the holiness of the mysteries celebrated
> there.

That relational, dialogical, and participative dynamism should con-
vince us that the altar does not stand in symbolic isolation, communicating solely to the assembly. This is where opening up the matrix of
symbolic relationships to include the other multivalent elements of the
environment becomes complex and also imperative. The placement of
the altar, focal as it is, cannot be designed without consideration of the
other four environmental sites.

We will add the ambo now to the creative conversation, considering its relationship to the altar as the central focus toward which the
assembly's sacramental activity spirals. The nourishment the table provides is itself a response to the word passed on as a "living and active,"
a fiat to the revelation of God's communication event with the people
of God who are convicted by the promise proclaimed there. To complete this dynamism, *the font and arrangement of the assembly* will then
be invited into the perichoretic dance that liturgy embodies, in "the
grace of our Lord Jesus Christ, the love of God, and the communion of
the Holy Spirit" that animates them. In truth, the altar is a nourishing
oasis on the journey into the arms of God, but everything else (ambo,
seating, lighting, et al.) "converges" there, as Albert Rouet reminds
us. This tensive relationship is important to the environment with a
name and a face, because the "Space as a Journey," Rouet insists, has an

itinerary that is eschatological. From that perspective, "the altar is not, however, the ultimate point of reference. The altar calls to mind the heavenly Jerusalem. There is something beyond the altar."[17] This is the eschatological promise of the Scriptures proclaimed and preached, and the ambo, to which we now turn, is its privileged vessel of reservation.

(b) The Word and Answer interchange is integral to what Otto Semmelroth calls "the redemptive dialogue" and animates the whole liturgical event.[18] It asserts that the *ambo* as the physical locus of the proclamation of the Scriptures be a revered place where the sacred story of the holy people is handed on and affirmed as "the Word of the Lord." GIRM 309 attests to its physical relationship to the sacramental Body at prayer:

> The dignity of the Word of God requires that in the church there be a suitable place from which it may be proclaimed and toward which the attention of the faithful naturally turns during the Liturgy of the Word....The ambo must be located in keeping with the design of each church in such a way that the ordained ministers and readers may be clearly seen and heard by the faithful.

Precisely how that sacramental site is positioned, the Instruction states, depends on the dimensions of the design and other uses of the worship space.[19] Common to all these diverse possibilities for configuration, the place of proclamation and preaching must remain a repository for the Scriptures, and not simply "a moveable lectern" that holds a book. This is because the ambo itself, within this relational dynamic, is a unique site of Christ's sacramental presence, as SC 7 insists. Its presence within the rhythm and harmony of the liturgy consecrates it with a vibrant resonance of its own, one from which the saving word takes on the living voice of both the tradition that has revered and canonized its testimony, as well as a living site where the unique resonance of a "fresh Word" for the assembly is uttered in this time and place.[20] Its summons leads the hearers to receive this testimony as the word of life here and now, "fulfilled in your hearing" (Luke 4:21). As the GIRM document says, the sacramental Body "naturally turns" toward this place in order to find her way toward the place of self-offering completed in the eucharistic mystery that unfolds and flows from this word. The *Pronotanda* for the *Lectionary for Mass* (LMI 10) signals at the outset the "essential bond" between word and table when the Holy Scriptures are read in the assembly:

> The Church is nourished spiritually at the table of God's word and at the table of the Eucharist: from the one it grows in wisdom and from the other in holiness. In the word of God the divine covenant is announced; in the Eucharist the new and everlasting covenant is renewed. The spoken word of God brings to mind the history of salvation; the Eucharist embodies it in the sacramental signs of the liturgy.

Consequently, as we mentioned concerning the altar, the ambo cannot stand alone, as in some nonliturgical ecclesial environments. For Roman Catholics and for all liturgical communities, the ambo itself represents a life-giving oasis that is leading *somewhere*. Without the reception of the summons the word offers in the proclamation event, the assembly cannot accept the shared vocation to join in Christ's self-offering at the table of the Eucharist and, as we echoed earlier from Augustine, "become what they receive." Regarding the proclaimed word and the sacramental actions that flow from that testimony and summons, the symbolic character of both the ambo and altar, to use Edward Schillebeeckx's imagery, "can be regarded simply as the burning focal points within the entire concentration of this visible presence of grace," bringing together the "inward and outward" communion with Christ the Head, with one another as the members of his Body, one voice proclaiming that grace to the entire world.[21] The spiral trajectory leads the assembly from feasting on the word, to the nourishing food of the altar, and on to the interior deepening of the bond with Christ and one another embodied in the communion procession. This necessitates that the place of proclamation be in active dialogue with all these rich proclamatory dimensions. The synergy in this movement ultimately directs the journey out the door into the hungry and thirsty world to which they have been sent, in the name and sacramental face of Christ to which eucharistic communion gives testimony.

In light of the honor due to this matrix of symbolic relationships, the safe and all-too-common practice of simply placing the ambo next to the altar in a confined sanctuary in the liturgical space may not be the best expression of that complex interrelationship between proclaimed word, shared meal, the taste of the fullness, and the communal mission.

Lex orandi, lex credendi, and *lex vivendi* are all influenced by the attentive intentionality of the ambo's placement.

If the proclamation and preaching of the word are part of the communal exercise of the praying assembly, where a shared text becomes a testimony with a name and a face, then *how* and *where* that occurs in mutual exchange with the sacramental Body becomes part of the word event as well. The "new hearing" that emerges when the place of proclamation communicates clearly the assembly's nearness to this word, affirming as well the communal identity embodied in receiving it "in her midst," naturally calls for a dignified place in relationship to the sacramental Body that reflects this multidimensionality of the sacredness of the word of God. Indeed, it encompasses the tradition handed down to them in faith and also communicates a here and now pathway of truth and life to those who open themselves to receive it. The ambo in truth is the communicative vessel of the sacramental grace that impels the ecclesial Body to carry this saving word out into that eschatological future toward which all liturgical praying tends. As the Letter to the Hebrews says,

> Therefore we must pay greater attention to what we have heard, so that we do not drift away from it....It was declared at first through the Lord, and it was attested to us by those who heard him, while God added his testimony by signs and wonders and various miracles, and by the gifts of the Holy Spirit, distributed according to his will. (Heb 2:1, 3b–4)

"Thanks be to God," the assembly responds upon hearing this. "Praise to you, Lord Jesus Christ," we acclaim. The Spirit-filled resurrected Body of Christ gathering to hear this saving word, invited then to eucharistic communion, joins in Christ's intimate relationship to the mission entrusted to him—his life, death, and resurrection—with all that entails in everyday living.

For this reason Jesus is not ashamed to call them brothers and sisters, saying, "I will proclaim your name to my brothers and sisters, in the midst of the congregation I will praise you." (Heb 2:11b–12) What stirs hearts at the ambo, then, cooperates in the invitation to the sacramental intimacy of the Body of Christ, Head and members, sinews joined together by God's promise fulfilled in the incarnate Word made flesh. This communication event gives flesh and voice to the Psalmist's claim, "We ponder your steadfast love, O God, in the midst of your temple" (Ps 48:9).

Some conclusions regarding the ambo seem evident from all this. Its physical placement ought never to be an afterthought when designing the liturgical environment, if the assembly's role is considered essential. It should cooperate with the synergy of place and people and purposeful action—human and divine—that flows through the praying. Surely its presence should be easily visible to all and enable a clear hearing of what is proclaimed there (GIRM 309), but the dynamism of the sacramental activity suggests a more creative possibility. Its placement in close relationship to the *communitas verbi*, a place within rather than set apart, may more easily "speak to" and engage the sacramental Body gathered for the communal narrative of salvation. A way to imagine this physical dynamism is the telling of a familial story around a fire or in a "living room," in the best sense of that term. Those who speak these narratives do not stand at the threshold of the assembled hearers and speak from beyond some secured boundary.

As a Spirit-embraced Body called to enact the saving mysteries that seal their identity in Christ and with one another, the place where the word of God finds its voice should be situated, in a very real sense in a way that expresses clearly that what is revealed there truly is "living and active...[and] able to judge the thoughts and intentions of the heart" (Heb 4:12). Because this liturgical setting is communal, and the hearts and ears that hear the word are, first and foremost, a unity of mind and body and spirit, we can argue that a revered placement *within the gathered assembly* seems appropriate.

Why do the logistics of space matter here? A reciprocal relationship between the ambo and the singular vessel that holds its message in communal embrace nudges the hearers in a way that an individual's reading of a text or one administered from a distant place cannot. The reader or preacher is able see the faces of those gathered to listen, turning and acknowledging the whole while honoring each one. At the same time, the ambo, as the GIRM says, should have a dignified bearing "suitable for the proclamation of the word" toward which the assembly's attention is intentionally "turned." This requires *solidity and beauty of design*, in a placement that highlights the beauty of the book and the place, but also ritually embraces the holy people who gather to receive it. Even more, the ambo as an engaged actor in this event should be able *to relate symbolically to the altar table as well*, the place

120

upon which the Body of Christ finds herself in union with Christ. As Wedig and Vosko note,

> The ambo is more than a pulpit or lectern and for that reason is better appreciated as second table…(and) should be understood as a table for the Word, and the locus for proclamation and preaching. Here a unique modality of Christ's presence is encountered in the Word. Therefore the dignity of the ambo should reflect the unique ministry of the Word that takes place in it.[22]

All of this taking place *matters* and it *forms* a people uniquely God's own. As the Letter to the Ephesians affirms,

> In him you also, when you had heard the word of truth, the gospel of your salvation, and had believed in him, were marked with the seal of the promised Holy Spirit; this is the pledge of our inheritance toward redemption as God's own people, to the praise of his glory. (Eph 1:13–14)

The wholeness of the liturgy as God's promise and fulfillment in Christ, and the wholeness of the assembly as primary celebrant, suggest the intimacy between these two liturgical tables. Indeed, Louis-Marie Chauvet, in *Symbol and Sacrament*, notes how the Bible as Sacred Scripture was birthed in the liturgy itself and "liturgy is the 'place' of Scripture" that "opens up sacramentality from the inside."[23] The eventfulness of reading the texts within the believing assembly canonized them in a real way before any institutional validation occurred. And so, both the Liturgy of the Word and the Liturgy of the Eucharist together formed and shaped the assembly of worshipers gathered. We can truly say, then, that the ambo and the altar are in conversation with the sacramental Body in a mutual exchange of gifts. Their complementarity represents what Otto Semmelroth, SJ, called "a single work" bestowing grace.[24] And so, as Chauvet goes on, "The Christian assemblies, Eucharistic and baptismal, seem to have functioned empirically as the *decisive crucible where the Christian Bible was formed*." Quoting the French biblicist C. Perrot, Chauvet concurs with him that the memorial Eucharist "is the place par excellence where the evangelical composition of history was crystallized. The gospel read in the Eucharistic celebration was born out of this celebration itself."[25] The ambo as a sacramental site is the focal site of a proclamation that always is leading *somewhere*. In a meaningful poetic description, Chauvet goes on to speak of this interrelationship of present, past, and future that the word engages in sacrament by saying, "the letter is always in transit" and "it is a letter stretched between the past it recounts and the future it announces… a present in the present."[26] And the proclaiming and hearing of the praying assembly are the embodied mediators of that Word-Sacrament connection, where the word handed on (and, therefore, grace-filled in itself and not subject to the assembly's whim) meets the sacramental Body hungering for communion with her Lord. To quote Chauvet,

> To the resistance of the letter, the rites add that of the body; the *letter-as-sacrament precipitates itself into the body-as-sacrament* in the expressive mediations of the rites: gestures, postures, objects, times and places, people with different roles.…*From the table of the Scriptures to the table of the sacrament* the dynamic is traditional and irreversible.[27]

Practical ways to fulfill these dynamics, as was mentioned, vary with culture and physical space, but creative possibilities emerge when the role of the ambo within the sacramental Body that treasures it is taken seriously. A placement from within the Body that communicates integrally with a centrally focused altar can occur in a space where *an antiphonal style allows altar and ambo to speak to each other* from anchored positions at each end. It can also be part of a placement where *the altar is in the center of the spiral and the ambo sits at one of the focal corners* to relate to the altar and to gathered assembly as a privileged locus of the presence of Christ, along with the presider's chair, the bishop's cathedra, and the cantor's raised setting adding to the other foci.[28] The importance here is that the environment in which the ambo, as the dignified and beautiful place where the word of God is proclaimed, must be a central conversation partner when the ritual celebration in which Christ is both Word and Answer reverences the praying Body as the primary celebrant of the sacred mysteries unfolding there. Creativity and diversity offer many possibilities, for indeed, as *Sacrosanctum Concilium* 123 articulated at the outset of the reform of the rites, "The Church has not adopted any particular style of art as her very own; she has admitted styles from every period according to the natural talents and circumstances of peoples, and the needs of the various rites."

One could even argue that the current state of ennui regarding the role of preaching and the proclamation of the word can be addressed by taking into consideration how the physical site of the ambo can encourage or mute sacramental engagement. A lack of intentionality in this regard can foster the attitude of giving a talk at a lectern rather than breaking open a revelatory word "fulfilled in the Body's hearing." As Richard Vosko has noted concerning its importance and the insufficiency of attention given to this proclamatory event, "A dualistic spiritual sensibility dividing this world from the next still hovers over contemporary Catholic preaching, devotional life, and theological reflection." As with all the sites of sacramental presence, he goes on to insist that "a greater bond between mind and body would eliminate dualism," which can make such an intimate relationship between Tradition and the living tradition embodied in the sacramental Body harder to appropriate.[29] Admittedly, an ambo alone does not put words into a preacher's mouth. However, when its setting and relationship to the other symbolic subjects at play are part of a larger conversation about the locus of the scriptural word within the liturgy, the dynamism taking place when "the holy scriptures are read in the Church" (SC 7) begins to be seen in its rich multidimensionality as a communication event of the "one whole Word of God." Its placement, we could insist, "speaks volumes." Given this, we can move on and widen the space in which the assembly engages these sacred mysteries. Anchored by the placement of altar and ambo, we will explore how the place of baptism as a primary site of focal presence finds its proper role in the house of prayer for the people of God.

(c) Given the ecclesial understanding of sacramentality and the mutual sharing of gifts we have discussed, the environment of the "tomb and womb" of *the baptismal font* and its role in liturgical praying deserves closer attention. Clearly, the place of baptism is not simply for Sunday afternoons and a private family gathering for a christening. Without a doubt, the font as primordial symbol is the hospitable threshold into this sacramental life for each individual bathed there. By means of each personal testimony, all who enter those saving waters, whether infant or adult, are literally bathed and embraced by the sacramental Body who receives them. They join in the communal call to share their gifts "to equip the saints for the work of ministry, for building up the body

123

of Christ" (Eph 4:12), in timeless communion with all who have gone before her in faith.

Through the grace of union with Christ and the Church—the *res tantum* of the sacrament—the baptized hopefully will recognize the font as the communal well of an ongoing ecclesial identity and life. The centrality of the baptismal pool speaks the same name and face to all and is the reason for the singular vessel of devotion to continue to engage the symbolic power resonant there: "In the same instant you died and were born again; the saving water was both your tomb and your mother," as Cyril of Jerusalem preached to the neophytes in the fourth century.[30] The end of a life apart and a birth to a new sacramental Body in Christ is the heart of what happens there and imprints its "character" on the assembly that worships within that renewing grace. "Baptism becomes the cradle of life," as Albert Rouet calls the sacrament event, for "a people baptized for the work of praise."[31]

Such fertility is affirming and challenging in its dangerous memory that consecrates, shapes, and forms the sacramental Body with ever new challenges for lives seeking wholeness. What happens to the neophytes in the baptismal pool continually refreshes, in a real way, the "cradle of life" for the whole sacramental Body journeying toward the fullness it signals. The neophytes stepping into the font and being raised up signals the beginning that prefigures the end for all of us together. Its flowing water speaks to both life's chaos and the generativity of laying down one's life "in order to take it up again" (John 10:17)—at one's initiation primally, but then, out of fidelity to Christ's own pasch, a continual surrender, a daily reorientation, an Easter event whose fifty days of feasting is the figurative ongoing capstone for the whole assembly. What is proclaimed for each at baptism is announced for all, because "they are us."

The font, then, is the multivalent symbol of the unity of the Body in Christ, who is "the gate" through which the baptized "will come in and go out and find pasture" (John 10:9b). This ritual pattern of washing and cleansing is transformative, and the font is its monument and invitation for all who enter and leave the house of prayer, who are baptized and buried as members of this Body, and who renew their identity in the waters of the font every time they dip their hands and sign themselves in the triune name. The rhythm and harmony of this never-ending perichoretic dance of initiation tones the entire sacramental Body in her prayer, the exercise of the "already and the not-yet"—a birth into a saving death that raises up to new life, only to return to the tomb to await the fullness of life. The continual eddying of those waters gradually hones the sacramental Body into the image of Christ the Head.

It is because of this continually renewed formative act that the "Introduction" to *Christian Initiation* 25 says, "The baptismal font... should be worthy to serve as the place where Christians are reborn in water and the Holy Spirit." The physical relationship between the font and the people of God who live in this environment must reflect this foundational identity and mission, embodied in these mysteries of gathering to "worship the Father in spirit and in truth." From its source waters and rippling out to all that gather there, the grace of this font is unleashed so that Jesus's words at the Samaritan well become the wellspring of everything else that occurs in worship and life: "Jesus said to her, 'I am he, the one who is speaking to you'" (John 4:26). The baptismal font speaks and beckons and sustains; that is why its placement within the liturgical environment—in relation to Word and table and those who feast there—demands attention and orients the rest of the sacred space and baptizes it as "holy."

Because the place of baptism is a privileged site of action and reflection, fidelity to the tradition augmented by a Spirit-filled imagination are necessary partners in any considerations regarding its placement within the liturgical environment. As a focal site in a mutual sharing of gifts, the font's relational, dialogical, and participative quality should be powerfully resonant and appropriate to the uniqueness of this community's name and face. As the *Book of Blessings* 1085 clarifies in practical detail, which artists and pastoral planners then take up in order to fashion a sacramental site for the local community, there are still ecclesial expectations for its design:

> The baptismal font, particularly one in a baptistery, should be stationary, gracefully constructed out of suitable material, of splendid beauty and spotless cleanliness; it should permit baptism by immersion, whenever this is the usage. (*Christian Initiation*, General Introduction, no. 25). In order to enhance its force as a sign, the font should be designed in such a way that it functions as a fountain of running water; where the climate requires, provision should be made for heating the water. (Ibid, no. 20).

Establishing the baptismal font's dignity and placement as worthy of foremost consideration, we will add to the conversation the sacramental Body that engages the font, both in baptism and in the everyday leading of a baptized life. The assembly's relationship to this site of focal presence will highlight how the font as a living symbol speaks and brings together and crystallizes that community's identity. Such a symbolic interchange, as Chauvet reminds us, "situates the Body as a 'subject,' with its cultural 'world,' in relation with other 'subjects,'" and, as with all symbols, particularly focal ones like the font, "'speak' to us before we even begin to talk."[32]

What precisely does the font "speak," simply in its focal placement? Lutheran theologian Maxwell Johnson has articulated eight "implications" for a spirituality rooted in the practice of Christian baptism.[33] Of particular relevance to this discussion is his claim that what happens at the font gives expression to a "re-claiming of baptism as the radical equalizer." Further, it reminds the assembly that this offer of life and redemption is a gift freely given ("a renewed stance against creeping Pelagianism"), and that the ministry of the Church that flows from its summons embraces the gifts of both lay and ordained members of the Body, for all were sealed and "characterized" there.[34] The event of baptism, symbolically and consistently expressed in the font, cannot find its fullest embodiment when ushered away to a side room in a quiet and empty church, for it "speaks" of the whole of life, what Johnson calls the "renewed sense of all Christian life as a living out of baptism" and "the practice of the communion of the baptized" at *all* levels of Christian life. Furthermore, from his Protestant perspective, the increase in ecumenical zeal—for the efficacy of baptism embraces all denominations bathed in the triune name—becomes a persistent and unending goad toward christic and ecclesial wholeness. *Ut unum sint...* (John 17:21).

This testimony of the font architecturally assists in breaking down the barriers of insiders and outsiders that an overly hieratic environment often "speaks," whether intended consciously or not. Liturgical architect Richard Vosko, in a recent book arguing for a worship environment that is both transcendent and immanent for the engagement of the liturgical assembly and her leaders in a mutually affirming way, reminds us, quoting the 2018 Pritzker Award Recipient, Balkrishna Doshi, "Architecture is not a static building—it's a living organism."[35] The font is a primordial witness to this. Throughout his study, Vosko

126

maintains that the gathered assembly, in consort with her leaders, finds its true home in a relational environment flowing from a common ecclesial identity. Speaking of the baptismal roots of this radical egalitarianism that still honors place and roles precisely in its common identity, he notes,

> The worship of God, an act of sacrifice and thanksgiving, is carried out through ritual action. The entire congregation enacts the liturgy; not just a few. This gathered cohort, by definition, is already the substantial Body of Christ by its baptism. The liturgy may continue to transform the assembly, inspiring it to work for justice and to reconcile itself with others. However, liturgy is not a quantifiable vessel of grace that is delivered by mediators as if they, the members, were not chosen for a purpose beforehand. Liturgical rituals are affirmations that something holy and extraordinary is already going on in the life of an individual and a community. Worshiping together raises the awareness of these epiphanies that border on God.[36]

The beauty and dignity of the font, therefore, honors the pivotal role that baptism plays in the rest of sacramental and ecclesial life in the midst of the world. It is here at this focal site that the assembly's baptismal identity is sacramentally sealed. As the Eucharistic Prayers for Various Needs acknowledge, the foundation of this name and face is its common origin in God, "You…who love the human race and who always walk with us on the journey of life." It is because the people of God pass through the waters of this font that the assembly can now gather as one Body "through him, with him, and in him," the Lord Christ, who is, as the Prayer continues,

> present in our midst when we are gathered by his love
> and when, as once for the disciples, so now for us,
> he opens the Scriptures and breaks the bread.[37]

The expansion of the relationship between the font, the ambo, and the altar irrevocably binds them together as focal sites that together body forth the relationship between Head and members, who together are *totus Christus*, the hope and promise of each one's baptismal identity.

The proclamation inherent in this symbolic exchange speaks of this identity before any catechesis crystallizes it. It "situates the Body as a subject within this sacramental world," to echo Chauvet,[38] and allows the assembly to speak truth about what happens in this space that has an ecclesial name and face.

Given the richness of these multivalent symbolic relationships, where then should the font best be placed to express this reality in Christ? Surely, the entrance to the worship space puts this primal relationship front and center. Another option is in the center of the seated assembly, where worshipers can engage it and each other during a baptismal rite and experience baptism coming out of the faith tradition embodied there. As the *Christian Initiation Pronotanda* (no. 25) suggests, its *dignity and beauty* should accompany its *usefulness* as a place of immersion and communal gathering. Holy water fonts for daily immersion, for example, would be more symbolically transparent when they spill into a larger pool of bathing and allow space to give the paschal candle its rightful place nearby outside the Easter season. To communicate its role in characterizing a living faith, to echo the documents cited above, water that is moving and flowing can enhance the clarity of its proclamation. Again, the particularities of architectural layout call for different options, but the intentional care for the construction and placement of a vibrant baptismal font cooperates in shaping a sacramental Body's ongoing ecclesial identity. As active agent and part of a "living organism," as Dashi the architect reminds us, the font communicates at primordial human levels—both inside and outside—that identity with Christ and one another that welcomes the ambo and the altar as partners in giving a name and a face to that communion of Head and members that is celebrated there. Honoring this emerging sacramental matrix, the final two focal sites, the place of the presider and the arrangement of the worshipers, can easily find their places as active subjects who live in this dwelling place of praise and thanks.

(d) The question of *the place of the presider* raises many issues of ecclesial identity, both for the assembly and the ordained leader who represents Christ the Head and the unity of the members he gathers. In a previous work, I argued for the meaning of Christ's sacramental presence in the presider by employing the image of "the gatherer of the community into communion."[39] This shifts the issue of the identity and function of the ordained minister from a "distinct and separate" mediator of the mysteries of faith or overseer of the Body to one charged with the charism of drawing the assembly to pray as "one Body, one Spirit in Christ." From this perspective, the heart of the presider's role comes first from *within* the sacramental Body, and its outward manifestation should reflect that kenotic role. Taking seriously this sacramental identity and function in the placement of the presider's chair helps to imagine how that is best expressed in a variety of options and architectural environments of different sizes and shapes. To ground those choices, we will first examine the identity of the leader of prayer vis-à-vis Christ and the sacramental Body. Next, how that identity (*in persona Christi*) is validated and expressed in leading the assembly as a gatherer of the community into communion (*in persona ecclesiae*) will highlight the role of the worshiping assembly as the primary celebrant of the liturgy and the presider's important gift of serving and facilitating that unity in the Body. The best in a variety of options for the placement of the presider's chair will then be evident.

The *sacramental identity of the presider*[40] always begins in an intentional acknowledgment that the trinitarian communion is its pattern and manner of presence. Sacramentally, Christ does not act alone, but always in communion with the Father in the power of the Spirit. The same is true for the presider who acts in the place and person of Christ, never alone but always in communion. Liturgical presidency, therefore, is a response to a "charismatic gift of grace," given to the one called and received humbly as gift and not as a right. Just as Christ accepted his mission from the gratuity of the Father's love, which is then poured out upon the beloved in the hallowing of the Spirit, the same is true for the gatherer of the community in the name of Christ, the Head of the Body.[41] Second, if the sacramental Body is the primary celebrant of the liturgy, then the presider's identity acting *in persona ecclesiae* is much like that of the conductor of a symphony, where the ensemble playing as one orchestra requires a mutuality between those who play the music and the skilled intentionality of the one who leads it.[42] The presider stands in this matrix of symbolic relationships as a sign of its covenantal bond in Christ.

The *liturgical function of gathering the community into communion* flows from this trinitarian foundation. How the presider presents himself—how he acts and leads—finds its effective embodiment in the way and truth and life of Jesus. This sacramental mode of Christ's presence is the incarnate expression of that redemptive relationship of Head and members bodied forth in the sacraments, especially in the

129

Eucharist. From this perspective, one does not preside "over" but gathers from "within." This, in turn, guides the decision of placement of this focal site of relational identity between Christ and the sacramental Body. It should respect the dynamism that all are acting subjects in this sacramental encounter. However, at the same time, as a unique and visible expression of the presence of Christ, the presider's chair should distinguish itself in that role of unifying the whole, allowing the entire assembly to see and hear the presider who gathers them.

Debates rage about whether a seat in the assembly or at a specific presider's chair set apart does justice to and best expresses both the identity and the function of the liturgical presider. The assumption offered here affirms the sacramental role of the presider, who, to use David Power's words, "represents Christ in community and sacrament," and to whom Susan Wood refers as "the representative sign and symbol of the unity of the community."[43] In both cases of standing in the midst of Christ and the Body, the relational, dialogical, and participative elements of liturgical presiding would suggest a placement that ensures that the gatherer be able to see and engage the assembly in its unity as an integral Body at prayer. A presider's chair sequestered in a barricaded sanctuary does not seem adequate to express this identity and function. And yet, seated merely as one worshiper among many in the assembly mutes that role of gatherer as well. Attentive intentionality grapples with this liminal role and decides accordingly. Some suggestions from a wide range of options flow out of this christic and ecclesial relationship that facilitates eucharistic communion and enables the singular vessel of devotion to pray with the wholeness of a sacramental Body united with her Lord and each other.

We can conclude that the presider's chair should have the same dignity and beauty as the font. It is not a throne, but neither is it a random place to sit. The presidential chair should create a symmetry between ambo and altar, where the presider gradually orchestrates this proclaiming and hearing of the word and the self-offering at the table with Christ that completes the redemptive dialogue. The often-seen horizontal lineup of ambo, altar, and presider's chair facing out to the assembly does little to express or embody that complex matrix of symbolic relationships and vibrant rhythm and harmony the liturgy as a whole promises. Once again, the particularities of space, the size of the gathering, and contextual considerations of cultural expressions of leadership all play a role in the placement and style for the presider's chair. An ecclesial understanding of sacramental presidency bodies forth the "mystery of Christ and the real nature of the true Church" and, as the Vatican II reform of the liturgy envisioned, "shows forth the Church to those who are outside as a sign lifted up among the nations under which the scattered children of God may be gathered together, until there is one sheepfold and one shepherd" (SC 2). Such liturgical intentionality in the environment allows for a placement that honors the relational identity and function of an ordained presider (*in persona Christi capitiis*), who is the gatherer of the Body and representative sign and symbol of their unity (*in persona ecclesiae*). He is summoned by the people of God to animate them as the *ekklesia*, the primary celebrant of the liturgy. Different options are possible, but the communicative intention of its placement must be clear. When all of these factors are reverenced, the place of the presider's chair "feels right" and the communion it symbolizes is tasted in a very real way.

(e) Given the environment that has been set, the *arrangement of the assembly at prayer* now humanizes the worship environment that has a name and face. The contours of the discussion flowing from this mutual sharing of gifts has a distinct clarity: the sacramental Body with a communal baptismal identity assembles into one place, hears and receives the word, intercedes in one voice, and shares in the self-offering at the table. The arrangement for the assembly as primary celebrant, therefore, engages all these focal points. The common practice of rows of pews or chairs facing in the same direction toward a set-apart sanctuary of chair-ambo-altar, as is all too common, does not honor who the assembly is when gathered together, nor does it enable the postures, gestures, voice, and processional movement to happen with ease. As Albert Rouet has called the interaction of liturgical subjects and their environment, "Sacred space is that of God's nomads. This itineracy is an important characteristic of those who seek God, of those who are members of the People of God."[44] There should be space to engage this symbolic, itinerant procession of the community in the midst of their lively journey into the wholeness the sacramental life offers. With all the focal points of Christ's presence in this sacramental encounter, the arrangement of a praying assembly comes alive and is "epiphanic," as Rouet goes on to say, and in this manifestation, truly a "place of encounter."[45]

Affirming this perspective, ease of seeing and hearing, admirable and necessary as they are, are only part of the picture. What is needed are transparent arrangements, such as circular or antiphonal seating, assisting the levels of symbolic communication to flow with clarity and ease. For example, Richard Vosko suggests that *circularity or seating around a central axis* "can promote and sustain relationships and communication with one another, with nature, and with God."[46] And responding to the argument that the eschatological symbolism of "a single of direction toward a transcendent God" should be maintained (the gist of the *ad orientum* argument), Vosko maintains,

> The counterpoint to this dualistic explanation is that the Body of Christ is already really present in the people gathered to celebrate the Paschal event that is theirs as a gift from God. In this case, the entire Church building, a metaphor for the People of God, is designed to convey both the immanent and transcendent presence of God as one holistic experience. God is neither here nor there but everywhere, even though many people have not noticed.[47]

Architecture, he concludes, can still enhance that immanence and transcendence of God, and that precious value can easily be imagined "where clergy and laity are gathered together all around the altar directly beneath the dome." It takes creativity to honor both the spoken and unspoken language of a liturgical environment that lifts up the heart and deepens the communion between Head and members. Vosko calls this "a place or an experience that is not *beyond* them as much as it is found *within* them."[48] This expresses a devotion from the inside out.

Another arrangement that evokes much interest and has been used for generations in monastic prayer settings is the *antiphonal seating for the assembly*. The proclamation and response nature of the liturgy and the mutuality of the "redemptive dialogue" as Word and Answer is not a peripheral consideration. It must be acknowledged that such engagement of members of the assembly with each other, who together are in relationship to both the ambo and the altar, may be uncomfortable to many, especially after many years of ritual scripting. But perhaps this discomfort is a challenging gift and not a barrier. Liturgical scholar Joyce Ann Zimmerman, CPPS, addresses this challenge to the assembly's common identity as a sacramental Body at prayer:

Some people object that seeing others during Mass is distracting. Perhaps this objection points to how little understanding we have of ourselves as the Body of Christ; how little regard we have for the inherent dignity of others; and how little we understand full, conscious, and active participation. Rather than a distraction, other people are fellow pilgrims on our journey toward salvation. We journey to eternal life together.[49]

Over time, the challenging gift could be a catalyst for a deeper communion unfolding in this sacred place, one that is epiphanic and resonant with the ubiquitous grace of God moving in synergy in the many languages of the sonorous space. Floorplans or explanations cannot convey this beforehand. This graced reality unfolds in the *doing* of communal prayer and not in prescriptions. Praying regularly together as a singular vessel of devotion in such an environment communicates the relationship in this Divine-human redemptive dialogue that finds its symbolic voice in the communion between Head and members, the *totus Christus* embodied in this time and place.

The varieties of possibilities, as we have noted,[50] are as diverse as the space and people and cultural expressions that make up the sacramental Body. Gathering, processing, listening, and raising minds and hearts together as one at the table are the primary actions of the celebrant of the Church's liturgy. The arrangement of the assembly goes a long way in allowing that encounter to happen and to shape the identity of the sacramental Body so that she processes out into the world to transform our common earthly dwelling into an environment that shares the features of this holy space with a treasured name and a face.

(2) *The identity-making responsibility on the part of the assembly to do the "work" of making a sacred space her own*—Liturgical spaces that house the sacramental Body do not simply emerge *ex nihilo*. As we have seen, creating a dynamic relationship between the focal sites where Head and members encounter the synergy of Word and Sacrament is not only the task of those who design and prepare sacred spaces. It is also the work of those who pray within its walls. The liturgical environment is a gift to the Body and the Body makes the sacred space holy. The holiness comes in the *being and doing* of the sacramental Body, who exercises her limbs and voice to proclaim God's saving acts in Jesus.

The gift given is first expressed through the care that is given to the design and the orchestrated use of its worship space, but to become truly the assembly's dwelling, there needs to be an attentive intentionality on the part of the sacramental Body to receive the space and make it her own. The journey then deepens and the sacramental identity matures in the responsibility the assembly assumes to do the redemptive "work" of liturgy in union with her Lord. This singular vessel of devotion, week after week, bears the spices of her praying to anoint the walls anew, much as the rite of dedication enacts.[51]

Jean Corbon imagines the ascension as the festal celebration of this shared labor that true worship "in spirit and in truth" entails. Christ still waits at the well to meet us and quench our thirst in the heat and weariness of our everyday lives.[52] The ascension is that pivotal handing over where Christ, present in the resurrected power of the Spirit, entrusts the sacramental Body with her mission "until all of us come to the unity of the faith and of the knowledge of the Son of God, to maturity, to the measure of the full stature of Christ" (Eph 4:13). In the ascension, as Corbon says, "The Lord has not gone away to rest from his redemptive toil; his 'work' (John 5:17) continues, but now at his Father's side, and because he is there he is now much closer to us, 'very near to us,' in the work of the liturgy of the last times."[53] In her practice of communal prayer, over time, the worshiping community must choose to allow the interior spirit of unity her baptismal identity pours out upon her to resonate with the physical space that holds her in this time and place. In both the conscious and unconscious appropriation of the environment of wood and stone and steel, she cooperates in fashioning the multivalent textures of this home where the Body of Christ recognizes herself bound to Christ and to each member of the *totus Christus*. In this unity of interior and exterior, the fashioner herself is shaped as a singular vessel of devotion and not simply a holding container for a hodgepodge of individual pious concerns. A consecrated people of God consecrates the space that continues to be "ever ancient and ever new."

This is not a "given"…it is work, the work of liturgy, the gracious work of the people in response to God's gratuitous redemptive work. Such sacramental transformation can only happen through the faithful and disciplined practice of prayer and praying together in this sacred space. It is the shared responsibility of the Body to make a home in which to dwell eucharistically, what Daelemans calls the assembly's *lived space*, where the rhythm and harmony of the liturgy can dance and sing.[54] When this happens, the environment resonates with the grace that flows there and nourishes the praying. Even a casual pilgrim visiting an empty church can sense this resonance, if the Body has done her work. Honoring that resonance elicits awe and a holy presence honoring the *totus Christus* who lives there.[55]

Such intentionality of ordinary practice within the space is often unnoticed and yet profound. Even the simplest of moments of encounter *matter* and they *form*. Passing by and immersing a hand in *the baptismal pool* or celebrating a rite of initiation is an invitation to bring together body and soul, mind and spirit, in a paschal identity that brings the dangerous memory of the dying and rising of Christ into every moment and person who gathers there. Every Sunday, poised as a *communitas verbi* for the word of God to be proclaimed and to listen together to its saving message, the assembly finds its interior harmony affirmed when the space acknowledges the dignity and beauty of *the ambo* and the *engaged seating* that confirms this as a shared event of proclamation. The response to the word of God leads to intercessory prayer within the Body. As we noted, all this ritual activity is leading *somewhere*. Recognizing that *the altar* is her sacramental center of self-offering and feasting testifies to the truth that turning now toward the table of the Lord happens from many directions, all drawn in synergy toward this focal site of eucharistic communion. As the first-century Didache prayer speaks from the interior dwelling of a common heart that honors the gathered Body dwelling now around the table, the presider intones,

> We give you thanks, Holy Father, for Your holy Name,
>   which you have made to dwell in our hearts....
> Remember, Lord, Your Church, to deliver it from all evil and
>   to perfect it in Your love;
> And gather it together from the four winds, sanctified for
>   Your kingdom
>   Which you have prepared for it;
> For Yours is the power and the glory for ever and ever.[56]

When this harmony of interior space meets the holy place of gathering, that name that dwells in the hearts of the faithful now bears its christic imprint upon every aspect of liturgical praying, and here in this place, truly has a face. This is the work of liturgy "in spirit and in truth."

(3) *Finally, the interaction of space, movement, and voice together coalesce to tap into the heart of the trinitarian communion that is her primary source and wellspring*—The symbolic language of liturgy, as we have maintained throughout, acknowledges the trinitarian communion as the source of all that happens in the space set aside for the singular vessel's devotion and prayer. When an assembly makes a home in a space, it is a gift given by the God who desires communion with the beloved Body who meets there. In that mutual interchange, this interior and exterior meeting renders it holy, an epiphany of graceful encounter through, with, and in Christ, and hallows the environment for worship as a place of pause and refreshment for the assembly as she journeys in the power of the Spirit to the fullness of the kingdom.

Albert Rouet spoke eloquently and yet simply about the role of liturgical architecture prepared for a praying assembly. "Christian space," he said, "is the space where transfiguration takes place."[57] Transfiguration, as spiritual writers have noted, is something that happens in the gospel to those who witness the glory that radiates on the face of Christ, reflecting the Father's own joy and the Spirit's fashioning of this redemptive plan, manifested in the conversation of Moses and Elijah with Christ on the holy mountain.[58] It is here that the disciples *see* their deepest identity expressed in this meeting of the humanity of Jesus with the divine glory, handed down through the ancestors in faith. But the point the Eastern writers make is that such humanness the Lord shares is not, in the end, "'being in a body,'...it means 'being a body,' an organic and coherent whole."[59]

That wholeness is a communion gift Christ shares with the Father and with the Church as the Spirit-filled resurrected Body of the Lord. "As the Father has loved me, so I have loved you; abide in my love" (John 15:9). The integration of an environment for the Body to express this trinitarian wellspring for her sacramental identity helps to give the space of worship this name and face. The persons of the Trinity do not act alone, but as a communion of persons, sharing love, being love, and hallowing every space with that love. The environment embodied in the focal sites that enhance Word and Sacrament needs a Body to make it holy. The inside and the outside, the interior unity and the unity of the space, sing a harmonic song when attention is given to its design and the practice within its walls. John Main's words at the opening of this chapter ring true once again about making a holy place for a holy people, and deserve a new hearing:

The first step in the creation of an environment for worship is therefore the sanctification of the hearts of worshipers or, rather, the realization of the holiness already there. This realization is achieved as they turn from self to God present in the faith of the community…a unique experience of Presence.[60]

Design styles and attitudes of what is sacred and beautiful can change, but the underlying role of the assembly as the primary celebrant of the liturgy and her gathering to hear the word and share the meal as a baptized people remains a strong foundational point of unity in Christ and one another. As Richard Vosko states about this seminal role of the place of worship,

In architectural terms, the identity of a church building may be classified as traditional, modern, or eclectic. But until the church building takes on the personality of a live congregation it lacks a "heart beat." It's just another structure, regardless of how it is categorized to style. What identifies a church as a servant in the community is not its architecture but the people who use the building.[61]

The "heartbeat" is the sign and symbol of a body's life. By extension, we have argued that the liturgical assembly as a singular vessel of devotion shares the characteristics of vibrant wholeness in mind and body and voice. The space, as we see, shares in that resonance of life-giving worship "in spirit and in truth." It is natural, then, that these reflections close with a concluding epilogue that returns to the heart, the wellspring, and the source of all communion. The Psalmist provides a prayer to make that transition:

How lovely is your dwelling place,
O Lord of hosts!

My soul longs, indeed it faints
for the courts of the Lord;

My heart and my flesh sing for joy
to the living God. (Ps 84:1–2)

EPILOGUE

The Heart of Christ: The Dynamic Center of the Singular Vessel of Devotion

> The Heart is Our Place—The outstreaming of the mystery
> of the liturgy into the rest of life begins in prayer, and the
> point where the river of life rises as a wellspring in the
> midst of human existence is the heart. It is through the
> prayer of the heart that liturgy becomes life.
>
> Jean Corbon, in *The Wellspring of Worship*[1]

A living body has a heart that beats, sending forth the life force from its center and receiving it back again to be renewed through its rhythmic pulse of life. In a similar rhythm and harmony, the mutual exchange of gift between the triune God and the worshiping sacramental Body of Christ follows a similar rhythm, a continuous dance of love *loving* and *being loved*, much as a heart circulates the lifeblood from its center to all the body's members and receives it back again.

Perhaps this is why the heart of Christ is such a powerful image in the Christian spiritual tradition. What is more, Christ and the Father share a communal heart out of which the Spirit energizes all creation. The Eastern Churches, we mentioned earlier, propose the primordial image of the Father's heart, pierced with love, which pours itself out upon the object of his thirst, in the self-offering of the only begotten

SINGULAR VESSEL OF DEVOTION

Son as an uttered Word of grace. In short, the trinitarian dynamism at work in us is a communal kenosis of self-emptying love. We share in this holy communion as a gift of the Spirit. As Corbon describes it, this is "the place where two pursuits, two thirsts meet, the place where two worlds, of grace and the flesh, intermingle."[2]

Returning to the heart of the sacramental Body at the end of this exploration of the unique aspects of the liturgical assembly is to return to the source and wellspring of all praise and worship. This heart of the sacramental Body finds its abundant life in communion with Christ, and in particular, the heart of Christ, whose saving mission finds its fulfillment by receiving divine love and offering it back to the Father in endless praise and thanks. As the sacramental Body of Christ, the *totus Christus* (Christ in us and we in him), our sharing in this mutual exchange of the life force unfolds. This embrace is the gracious gift of the Spirit, who hallows our own gifts and unites them to Christ's own self-offering to the Father.

Theologian David Fagerberg, using what he calls a "spatial metaphor" as an image of this interchange of energy, divine and human, describes the source of the dynamism at work. He notes that in the liturgy and the assembly at prayer, it is "as if in creation the Trinity turned itself inside out, and being was poured through the hierarchies as a golden chain from the Uncreated to the created." We breathe in and breathe out the very life of the source of all life. Fagerberg goes on to cite mid-twentieth century theologian and apologist Louis Bouyer to extend this metaphor. Bouyer describes the liturgical dynamic, "in which the triune fellowship of the divine persons has, as it were, extended and propagated itself," with the metaphor of "a beating heart." In the sacramental Body at prayer, this center finds its place in the gathered assembly of saints and angels around the throne of God singing the ancient hymn of praise. This liturgical heart "moves the ebb and flow of the creating *Agape* and of the created *eucharistia*," Bouyer affirms, and so he concludes,

> Thus this immense choir of which we have spoken, basing ourselves on the Fathers, finally seems like an infinitely generous heart, beating with an infinite diastole and systole, first diffusing the divine glory in paternal love, then continually gathering it up again to its immutable source in filial love.[3]

Throughout this book, the singular vessel of devotion in communal prayer has been shown to engage in this mutual indwelling at every dimension of her life, interior and exterior, gathered now as "one Body, one spirit in Christ." This indwelling embraces her communal attitude of a loving mind in union with Christ (Phil 2:2). Such a sacramental way of being spills over into her bodily movements in harmony with Christ as a true Body and mystical Body, a communion incarnate. This allows the timbre of her voice and the communal ear that receives and sings this praise and thanks to share a divine resonance of sacred speech. A communal devotion then is nourished, one that hallows the space in which she gathers to take on the name and face of Christ within "the household of God, which is the church of the living God" (1 Tim 3:15). Such is the embodied geography of worship these chapters have explored.

As a member myself of a sacramental Body in prayer, as well as one called as a presbyter to be embedded in her heart to gather the community into communion, I testify to the truth of the dynamism of this ebb and flow of grace whose wellspring is divine. In what the tradition calls the *kenosis* and the *ascension* (an *exitus* and a *reditus*),[4] whose "felt knowledge" can only happen in the *being* and the *doing*, a sacramental Body finds its true identity. The sacramental Body, like all bodies, requires care and nurture. An attentive intentionality that reverences this communion and calls the assembly to hand herself over as "one Body, one Spirit in Christ" only increases the graciousness of this holy communion. Breathing in and breathing out this life force allows the Body to be centered, held, and free. To affirm Corbon's image at the outset of this epilogue, "The Heart *is* Our Place."

As these chapters have hopefully conveyed, this is communal holiness in the flesh, pure gift, offered and received. It suggests a devotion that is inextricably communal. It is not simply a collection of individual pieties, but a new reality in communion with Christ and one another. There is no other way to explain what it means to pray together in this way, as if words could capture the ineffable mystery of what Bouyer describes as "the creating *Agape* and of the created *eucharistia*." Here we enter into the contours of prayer in the liturgical heart, always "through Him, with Him, and in Him, in the unity of the Holy Spirit, where all glory and honor is yours, Almighty Father, forever and ever." As a liturgical theologian, a member of the assembly, and its presider, I cannot explain it, but I would give my life for this Body, revealed, deepened, and drawing its life "when kindred live together in unity" (Ps 133:1). Its promise and gift is worth the vulnerable risk involved in being a singular vessel of devotion. The sacramental Body at prayer is the place of a living faith, and I see it alive in so many places where communities gather in fidelity to "do this in memory of Me." It is our legacy and our trust to keep this heart alive and circulating with fresh energy in these fractured times in which we live. We have a mission as a sacramental people moving toward the fullness of all things in Christ. This is God's redemptive way.

As I have paid attention and pondered this awesome mystery over the years, I believe the way of praying outlined in these pages forges a Christian identity that so many people hunger to embrace as their own, in hospitable union with all people and the diversity of faith paths. The primary signs and symbols the liturgy offers to "body forth" that identity, along with artful presiding and liturgical service, allows the Body, over time, to grow and thrive in this mission. That is our hope and the hope of this book. The rest is God's own work, and as the narrative of God's tender mercies in all generations attests, this God is faithful. God keeps God's Word. He keeps Christ close to his heart, and Christ's heart is now our life center. That is the liturgy's promise.

> For as the rain and the snow come down from heaven,
>   and do not return there until they have watered the earth,
> making it bring forth and sprout,
>   giving seed to the sower and bread to the eater,
> so shall my word be that goes out from my mouth;
>   it shall not return to me empty,
> but it shall accomplish that which I purpose,
>   and succeed in the thing for which I sent it. (Isa 55:10–11)

"What wondrous love is this, O my soul," the Church sings. The graciousness moving in and through the Body should call us to jubilant praise but also to a reverent silence. Our common worship asks us to exercise both dimensions, giving space and honor to each manner of expressing communal devotion.[5] In the course of my experience in the sacramental Body at prayer, everything matters and everything forms. Given its dynamism, the fashioned artwork of the singular vessel comes forth from the kiln as a new creation, a new reality, a people bound to Christ and Christ to her. Praise and silence speak volumes and exercise

142

the sacramental Body in their own unique ways. The Carmelite tradition calls this type of prayer a "divine apprenticeship, in which God's tenderness makes the soul, too, an expert in loving—*maestra de amor*."[6] The contemplative love song, the *Spiritual Canticle* of John of the Cross, born out of a suffering love in the manner of Christ, gives poetic utterance to the task of learning to love in the manner of Christ's own heart:

> So it is that the soul has been not only instructed in love; she has become an expert in loving, united with the expert himself, and, as a result, she has found fulfillment; fulfillment will be hers only when she comes to a love like this.[7]

Love as an abundant fulfillment is a perfect place to end. Loving as an integral action of mind and heart and body will remain "a still more excellent way" (1 Cor 12:31) for each beloved soul to be united both with Christ the lover and the sacramental Body, who together are the limbs and members of this holiness in our midst. It takes attention, a willingness, and a communal handing over to Christ, whose pierced heart—a mirror of his Father's—stands at the cosmic well and waits to receive us in his and our self-offering to the One who loved first. Truly, "The Heart is Our Place" and this singular vessel has a home. As we end all prayers and pleas, "Amen. So be it."

NOTES

PREFACE

1. See Henri de Lubac, "Mysticism and Mystery," in *Theological Fragments* (San Francisco: Ignatius Press, 1989), 56.

2. Jean Corbon, in *The Wellspring of Worship* (New York: Paulist Press, 1988), 17. In the outpouring of the Trinity's loving action in the resurrection, the wellspring of worship rises up from the depths of God. As Corbon says, "No longer will human beings worship here or in some place, because the Holy of Holies has now been unveiled: in the depths of the Father's torn heart," 30.

3. From St. Thomas Aquinas, "Pange Lingua, Gloriosi," Text 87 87 87, *Liber Hymnarius*.

4. This and all references to liturgical texts are taken from the English translation and chants of *The Roman Missal* (2010), International Commission on English in the Liturgy Corporation. All rights reserved.

5. St. Catherine of Siena, Letters, 49–50; see *Prayers of Catherine of Siena*, ed. Suzanne Noffke (New York: Paulist Press, 1983).

6. Alexander Schmemann, *For the Life of the World* (Crestwood, NY: St. Vladimir's Seminary Press, 1988), see 26–28.

7. Paul A. Janowiak, *The Holy Preaching: The Sacramentality of the Word in the Liturgical Assembly* (Collegeville, MN: Liturgical Press, 2000) and *Standing Together in the Community of God: Liturgical Spirituality and the Presence of Christ* (Collegeville, MN: Liturgical Press, 2011). Besides SC 7, see also the General Instruction of the Roman Missal (GIRM), e.g., nos. 3–5, 55, 95–96.

8. See, e.g., Bertrand Ruby, "Mary, A Model of Ecclesia Orans, in Acts 1:14," in *Marian Studies* 35, no. 12 (1984): 87–99.

CHAPTER 1

1. See, e.g., Louis-Marie Chauvet, *Symbol and Sacrament: A Sacramental Reinterpretation of Christian Existence*, trans. Patrick Madigan, SJ, and Madeleine Beaumont (Collegeville, MN: Liturgical Press, 1995), 151–55 and 182–85. and his *The Sacraments: The Word of God at the Mercy of the Body* (Collegeville, MN: Liturgical Press, 2001), 139–41. This intimate relationship is also explored in Goffredo Boselli, *The Spiritual Meaning of the Liturgy: School of Prayer, Source of Life* (Collegeville, MN: Liturgical Press, 2014), 118–26. They are building upon the work of many contemporary forebears, such as Henri de Lubac, I. M. Dalmais, and a host of mid-twentieth century sacramental theologians.

2. The glorified wounds of the risen Lord are singular marks of the truth of his victorious resurrection, inscribed on his own Body. See John 20:27, when Jesus invites Thomas to place his very hand in these wounds, saying, "Do not doubt but believe."

3. Chauvet, *Symbol and Sacrament*, 51. Following Heidegger and J.-L. Marion, Chauvet calls this conversion, an entrance into a dynamic presence that summons them to "let themselves go toward this demanding *letting be*" (surrendering control and handing oneself over to truly *be with* and *in* him). The sacraments are the "distinctive representations" and "the symbolic place where God becomes enfleshed in our humanity." This invitation to transformation of the community's sacramental identity was not a once and for all event of the postresurrection community. Nor is it an isolated moment in any assembly. The open-endedness, Chauvet says, is "a continual *advent* exposed to the risks of history and the Church's interpretive freedom under the Spirit's inspiration" (61). The identity of the sacramental Body is never fixed and stable, but always walking *toward* the fullness, with hands open and eyes to the horizon.

4. Chauvet, *Symbol and Sacrament*, 83.

5. For a rich and extended discussion of "mystical reality" and the "mystical body" in both a sacramental and ecclesial sense, see Henri de Lubac, *Corpus Mysticum: The Eucharist and the Church in the Middle Ages* (1st ed. 1939), trans. C. J. Gemma Simmonds et al., ed. Laurence Paul Hemming and Susan Frank Parsons (Notre Dame, IN: University of Notre Dame Press, 2006), esp. part 1, "The Evolution of the Sense of *Corpus Mysticum*."

146

6. Chauvet, in *Symbol and Sacrament*, calls this a dynamic and ever-deepening "'transitive' way," and, quoting Heidegger, says that "we have truly *heard* [*gehört*] when we *become part* [*gehören*] of what is spoken to us" (54). The speaking One speaks in and through us (42).

7. See *Lumen Gentium*, esp. nos. 7, 8.

8. Chauvet, *Symbol and Sacrament*, 147.

9. See Iain Matthew, OCD's description of the fountain flowing from the heart of God as a trinitarian event in *The Impact of God: Soundings from John of the Cross* (London: Hodder & Stoughton, 1995), 73. He describes it as "the Father surrendering to the Son, Son self-emptying to the Father, Spirit-water spilling out to create a universe; the cosmos comes to sip it, though all—heaven, people, hell—are already drenched in it." This trinitarian sharing of life shared is sealed and communicated at the Eucharistic table.

10. Rite of the preparation of the candle from the Easter Vigil in the holy night.

11. The dynamic character of the "Word of the Father" is rich in the tradition. Herbert Vorgrimler describes it simply as always communicated, a "saving event" tied now to the flesh of this material world in which what is communicated "effects what it says [and] brings what it announces." Hence, this relationality is never for itself alone; it is generative and never "self" contained. See Herbert Vorgrimler, *Sacramental Theology*, trans. Linda M. Maloney (Collegeville, MN: Liturgical Press, 1992), 77.

12. In an earlier book, *Standing Together in the Community of God*, I called this sacramental presence of Christ in the presider as that of a "gatherer of the community into communion." See ch. 4. By analogy, this interior attitude in the presider enables the interior of the gathered communion to coalesce; it is iconic as well. This will be discussed further in chs. 3 and 4.

13. "Gather Us In," text and music by Marty Haugen, 1979 (GIA Publications, 1982).

14. Sarah Coakley, *God, Sexuality, and the Self: An Essay on the Trinity* (Cambridge: Cambridge University Press, 2013), 13.

15. Gordon Lathrop, *The Pastor: A Spirituality* (Minneapolis: Augsburg/Fortress Press, 2006), 23–40.

16. C. S. Lewis, *The Last Battle*, vol. 7 of *The Chronicles of Narnia* (London: HarperCollins, 1998), 102–3.

17. The Prefaces of the Roman Missal, 3rd ed.

18. This paradox of the cross takes on the contours of Christ's Body, in what L.-M. Chauvet, in *Symbol and Sacrament*, calls "an event *within* God's own self" (498) and remarks that Walter Kasper captures this crucified Lord Jesus as one revealed as "a form hollowed out to receive the fullness of God." Walter Kasper, *Jesus the Christ*, 5th ed. (New York: Paulist Press, 1985), 177.

19. Chauvet, *Symbol and Sacrament*, 147; See also Chauvet's use of Merleau-Ponty's understanding of embodied "thought," esp. n7, 146.

20. *The Hiding Place*, 35th anniversary ed. (Grand Rapids: Chosen Books, 2006), 227.

21. Eucharistic Prayer 3 in the Roman Missal.

22. N.B. Luke 24:1–3 and the women who prepare the spices to anoint the body of the crucified Lord.

23. Penitential Rite I, Roman Missal, 3rd ed.

24. Invocation for the Penitential Act, Roman Missal, 3rd ed.

25. Coakley, *God, Sexuality, and the Self*, 13.

26. Chauvet, *Symbol and Sacrament*, 147.

27. Chauvet, *Sacraments*, xii.

28. David Fagerberg, *On Liturgical Asceticism* (Washington, DC: CUA Press, 2013), 123.

29. Chauvet, *Symbol and Sacrament*, 491.

30. See, e.g., Janowiak, *Standing Together*, 17, 92. This threefold character of the liturgy is a foundational principle of this previous book. It also profits from Edward Schillebeeckx's pioneering work on the historicity and corporeality of the Christ event as manifested sacramentally in the Church, accentuating the dynamism between the incarnate Christ and the concrete ecclesial assembly. E.g., in *Christ the Sacrament of the Encounter with God* (Kansas City, MO: Sheed and Ward, 1963), Schillebeeckx makes this point precisely:

> The man Jesus is the presence of the redeeming God among us, though in the mode of the human presence bodying that presence forth to us. Precisely for this reason the plan of incarnation requires, from the moment of Christ's ascension, a prolongation of his bodily mediation in time. We already know that this sacramental body of the Lord is the Church (59).

31. In the Exsultet on Easter night, the opening lines after the invitatory dialogue sing out this communal song of praise:

It is truly right and just, with ardent love of mind and heart
and with devoted service of our voice,
to acclaim our God invisible, the almighty Father,
and Jesus Christ, our Lord, his Son, his Only Begotten.

32. Paul's liturgical hymn in Phil 2:5–11 takes on particular significance in this light: humility, self-emptiness, profoundly human in his form, he becomes flesh as a fitting vessel that gives a name to this Body:

Therefore, God highly exalted him
    and give him the name
      that is above every name,
so that at the name of Jesus
    every knee must bend,
      in heaven and on earth and under the earth,
and every tongue should confess
    that Jesus Christ is Lord,
      to the glory of God the Father. (vv. 9–11)

33. Chauvet describes the "theological pertinence" of this dynamic of gift exchange in *Sacraments*, 123–27.

34. Lathrop, *The Pastor: A Spirituality*, 37–40.

35. Surely, the institution of the hierarchical Church is the structure of this evangelizing and prophetic community of faith. What is highlighted here is the interiority and devotional attitude of the people of faith. This ecclesial community exists and expresses her identity most transparently in her ritual celebrations as the Body of Christ. From this perspective, the two terms of *Church* and *sacramental Body* are, in a very real way, synonymous. *Lumen Gentium* speaks directly to this when it says that "the Church, in Christ, is in the nature of sacrament—sign and instrument, that is, of communion with God and unity among all [persons]" (no. 1). And later, the document says that such multidimensionality of the "visible society and the spiritual community, the earthly Church and the Church endowed with heavenly riches…form one complex reality which comes together from a human and a divine element" (no. 8). So to speak of "the Church" is not to imagine first the institutional, canonical, and hierarchical structures, although the whole certainly includes this, but the Spirit-filled resurrected Body of the Christ.

36. Chauvet, *Sacraments*, 32.
37. Coakley, *God, Sexuality, and the Self*, 13.
38. E.g, the *OED*.
39. LG 8. See n. 32.
40. Walter Kasper, "Die Kirche," cited in Vorgrimler, *Sacramental Theology*, 37.
41. See Susan Wood, *Spiritual Exegesis and the Church in the Theology of Henri de Lubac* (Grand Rapids: Eerdmans, 1998), 55.
42. LG 7, emphasis mine. The footnote for this passage in LG includes numerous references to this Spirit in the body analogy, including John Chrysostom, Thomas Aquinas, Leo XIII, and Pius XII.
43. See n. 42 and, for a fuller treatment of this, see Janowiak, *Standing Together*, 39–45.
44. Augustine, *Confessions*, bk. 10, ch. 27.

CHAPTER 2

1. Paul Evdokimov, *The Sacrament of Love: The Nuptial Mystery in the Light of the Orthodox Tradition* (Crestwood, NY: St. Vladimir's Seminary Press, 1985).
2. Bianco da Siena, 15th c. hymn to the Holy Spirit, "Discendi, Amor Santo" in his *Laudi Spirituali del Bianca da Siena*, trans. Richard Francis Littledale; set to music in most liturgical hymnals by Ralph Vaughan Williams (1872–1958).
3. See chap. 1, n. 41.
4. Preface 2 of the Ascension of the Lord, *Roman Missal*, 3rd ed.
5. Henri de Lubac, *Theological Fragments* (San Francisco: Ignatius Press, 1985), 72.
6. Preface 6 of the Sundays in Ordinary Time.
7. Henri de Lubac, "The Eucharist as Mystical Body," in *Corpus Mysticum: The Eucharist and the Church in the Middle Ages* (1st ed. 1939), trans. C. J. Gemma Simmonds et al., ed. Laurence Paul Hemming and Susan Frank Parsons (Notre Dame, IN: University of Notre Dame Press, 2006), 23.
8. For an extended discussion of the terms *corpus verum* and *corpus mysticum* and their shifting from what de Lubac called "symbolic inclusions" to "dialectical antitheses," see Paul A. Janowiak, *Standing*

150

Together in the Community of God: Liturgical Spirituality and the Presence of Christ (Collegeville, MN: Liturgical Press, 2011), 56–65.

9. de Lubac, *Corpus Mysticum*, 24.

10. Louis-Marie Chauvet, *The Sacraments: The Word of God at the Mercy of the Body* (Collegeville, MN: Liturgical Press, 2001), 38–39. I am indebted to this *mysterium fidei* that Chauvet describes in discussing the necessity of the ecclesial body as a mediating symbol of humanity's encounter with Christ and the primary celebrant of the liturgy in *Standing Together*, 47. The effect of this on the sacramental Body's self-identity and the role of the ordained presider is richly significant.

11. Alexander Schmemann, *For the Life of the World* (Crestwood, NY: St. Vladimir's Seminary Press, 1988), 26–27 (emphasis mine).

12. David Fagerberg, *On Liturgical Asceticism* (Washington, DC: CUA Press, 2013), 123.

13. Io. Ev. 26.13, 15.

14. *Liber de cardinalibus operibus Christi* (PL, 189, 1643–4); de Lubac, *Corpus Mysticum*, 192.

15. Ghislain Lafont, *Eucharist: The Meal and the Word* (2001), trans. Jeremy Driscoll, OSB (Mahwah, NJ: Paulist Press, 2008), 107, 110.

16. Lafont, *Eucharist*, 107, 110.

17. The Spanish renders the impelling nature of the liturgical deed with great clarity than the English, which is "right and just."

18. Lafont further distinguishes between ritual language and discourse that is "invocation" (addressed to) and "evocation," which, in the remembering, makes the current utterance an occasion for gratitude. See *Eucharist*, 43ff. Chauvet describes a similar dynamic in ritual language as communicative speech that is both "declarative and performative." See *Symbol and Sacrament*, 131–32.

19. Chauvet, *Symbol and Sacrament*, 163.

20. Chauvet, *Symbol and Sacrament*, 161; emphasis mine.

21. Chauvet, *Symbol and Sacrament*, 160.

22. Nathan Mitchell, *Meeting Mystery: Liturgy, Worship, Sacraments* (Maryknoll, NY: Orbis Books, 2006), 150.

23. Mitchell, "The Poetics of Space," reprinted in *At the Heart of the Liturgy* (Collegeville, MN: Liturgical Press, 2014), 14.

24. Yves Congar, "'Real' Liturgy and 'Real' Preaching" (1948), in *At the Heart of Christian Worship: Liturgical Essays of Yves Congar*, trans and ed. Paul Philibert (Collegeville, MN: Liturgical Press, 2010), 11.

25. *Roman Missal,* 3rd ed.

26. See, e.g., Rom 16:16; 1 Cor 16:20; 2 Cor 13:12; 1 Thess 5:26; 1 Pet 5:14.

27. For more on the notion of the word proclaimed and thereby forming "preached communities," see Paul Janowiak, *The Holy Preaching: The Sacramentality of the Word in the Liturgical Assembly* (Collegeville, MN: Liturgical Press, 2000), esp. 186.

28. See Karl Rahner, "The Word and the Eucharist," in *Theological Investigations,* vol. 4, trans. Kevin Smyth (New York: Crossroad, 1982), 267.

29. See GIRM 57.

30. Benedict XVI, *Sacramentum Caritatis,* no. 6.

31. Among many versions of this spiritual, see "Plenty Good Room," comp. and arr. by Rob Glover, in *Lead Me, Guide Me,* 2nd ed. (Chicago: GIA, 1987).

32. Tertullian, *De Carnis resurrectione,* 8: *Patrologia Latina* (*PL*), 2, 806.

33. See, e.g., 2 Sam 5:3; 1 Kgs 1:39; 1 Chr 16:22.

34. *Roman Missal,* 3rd ed.

35. Jean Corbon, *The Wellspring of Worship* (1980), trans. Matthew J. O'Connell (New York: Paulist Press, 1988), 109. A second English translation was published in 2005 by Ignatius Press, San Francisco.

36. Antonio Donghi, *Words and Gestures in the Liturgy* [Ital. ed., Libreria Editrice Vaticana, 1993] (Collegeville, MN: Liturgical Press, 2009), 52. This book is an excellent resource for a whole range of sacramental matter and form and the importance of honoring the distinct importance of each.

37. See Chauvet, ch. 4, "Symbol," in *Sacraments,* esp. 70–74.

38. For a description and history of the three types of holy oils— oil of catechumens, sacred chrism, and oil of the infirm, see the works of James Empereur, SJ, Gerard Austin, OP, Leonel L. Mitchell, Maxwell Johnson, and many others.

39. See nn. 22–23.

40. It is important to note that what was formerly considered "the last rites" has been reimagined to recover this eucharistic dynamism. Viaticum is now considered the final sacrament of the dying Christian. See the restored rite of anointing and viaticum in danger of death.

41. This imagery comes from the Methodist Eucharistic Prayers composed after the Vatican II reform.

42. GIRM 42, citing also SC 30, 34.

43. Romano Guardini, *Spirit of the Liturgy* (New York: Crossroad, 1998), 37.

44. Romano Guardini, *Sacred Signs* (St. Louis: Pio Decimo Press, 1955), 21, 22.

45. Donghi, *Words and Gestures*, 32.

46. See GIRM 42, 95–96 and *Summorum Pontificorum*.

47. See, e.g., Benedict XVI, *Sacramentum Caritatis* (2007), no. 52.

48. Susan Wood, *Spiritual Exegesis and the Church in the Theology of Henri de Lubac* (Grand Rapids: Eerdmans, 1998), 68. See also Janowiak, *Standing Together in the Community of God*, 46–51.

49. Guardini, *Sacred Signs*, 22.

50. The priest acts *in persona Christi* because he acts *in persona ecclesia*. See Janowiak, *Standing Together*, 129–56. Citations include such theologians as Wood, David Power, Thomas Rausch, Edward Kilmartin, and Kenan Osborne, all of whom have addressed the issue of *in persona Christi* out of an ecclesial context.

51. Guardini, *Spirit of the Liturgy*, 37; emphases mine.

52. Aimé Georges Martimort, ed., *The Church at Prayer: An Introduction to the Liturgy*, vol. 1, *Principles of the Liturgy* (Collegeville, MN: Liturgical Press), 180–81.

53. Dalmais, in Martimort, *Church at Prayer*, 1:181–82.

54. One could argue for prostration of all the ministers, lectors, and servers along with the presider on Good Friday precisely because of its communal significance of the community's identity with Christ. Prostration and standing actually complement one another and speak of the same communal mystery at the heart of the *totus Christus*.

55. Donghi, *Words and Gestures*, 34.

56. Donghi, *Words and Gestures*, 34.

57. Pope Francis, "Address to the Clergy in the Cathedral of San Rufino in Assisi, Italy, 4 October 2013," in *The Church of Mercy: A Vision for the Church* (Chicago: Loyola Press, 2014), 75.

58. Donghi, *Words and Gestures*, 36.

59. See n. 1.

60. Henri de Lubac, "Christian Community and Sacramental Communion," in *Theological Fragments* [*Théologies d'occasion*, 1984] (San Francisco: Ignatius Press, 1989), 72.

61. Lafont, *Eucharist*, 163.

62. This is the description of Gerard Manley Hopkins's form of poetry making. In his *Correspondence* 14, October 6, 1878, the Jesuit poet tells Richard Watson Dixon, "I had long had haunting my ear the echo of a new rhythm which now I realized on paper. To speak shortly, it consists in scanning by accents and stresses alone." Linguistic scholar Walter Ong writes of this in his essay "Hopkins' Sprung Rhythm and the Life of English Poetry (1941/1949)," in *An Ong Reader: Challenges for Further Inquiry* (Cresskill, NJ: Hampton Press, 2002), 111.

63. De Lubac, *Corpus Mysticum*, 197; emphasis mine.

CHAPTER 3

1. Ballad I: "In Principio" (On the Most Holy Trinity), *The Poems of John of the Cross*, trans. John Frederik Nims, 3rd ed. (Chicago: The University of Chicago Press, 1989), 47.

2. The eminent Jesuit linguistic scholar Walter Ong, SJ, speaks of language as "a very mysterious thing" and "creative in a distinctly human way. It directs [a person] beyond himself. It enables him to direct the things around him beyond themselves." See *Why Talk? A Conversation about Language with Walter J. Ong*, the National Humanities Faculty Why Series (Novato, CA: Chandler & Sharp Publishers, Inc., 1979), 1.

3. Included in this communication is a revered written text, the sharing of conversation, singing to another or together, as well as a host of similar speech acts, such as poetry reading, shared silence, verbal directions, etc.

4. Ghislain Lafont, *Eucharist: The Meal and the Word* (2001), trans. Jeremy Driscoll, OSB (Mahwah, NJ: Paulist Press, 2008), 43.

5. Karl Rahner uses this term to speak of the unifying actions and sacramental character of the Church, which are part of every utterance and action that go to make up her reality as a basic or fundamental sacrament. See his essay "The Word and the Eucharist," *Theological Investigations*, vol. 4, trans. Kevin Smyth (New York: Crossroad, 1960), esp. 279. Hence, word and table are both part of this "one whole Word of God," what he calls "an essentially envisaged whole," that announces the presence of "grace, reconciliation, and eternal life:

Jesus Christ." See Rahner, *The Church and the Sacraments*, trans. W. J. O'Hara (New York: Herder and Herder, 1964), 15.

6. I have used this term to speak of the surface words and pious platitudes that often take the place of true sacred speech, which wrestles with the scriptural warrant, the ambiguity of life, and the lukewarm faith that seeks to makes sense of the Christian message for the contemporary world today. See Paul Janowiak, SJ, University of Notre Dame 2016 Marten Lecture in Preaching, "Encountering a Laboring Word: From Idol Chatter to Holy Preaching."

7. See SC, nos. 1–2. The document speaks at the outset of an underlying premise for renewal and reform of corporate worship: "For the liturgy, 'through which the work of our redemption is accomplished,' most of all in the divine sacrifice of the Eucharist, is the *outstanding means* whereby the faithful may express in their lives, and manifest to others, *the mystery of Christ and the real nature of the true Church.*" The quote is from the Proper for the Ninth Sunday after Pentecost; emphases mine.

8. I borrow this image from Otto Semmelroth, SJ, *The Preaching Word: On the Theology of Proclamation*, trans. John Jay Hughes (New York: Herder and Herder,1965). This dynamic of "Word and Answer" will be discussed in further detail later in the chapter. See n. 17 below.

9. Herbert McCabe, "The Word of God," in *The New Creation* (New York: Continuum, 2010: Sheed and Ward, 1964), 3.

10. Lafont, *Eucharist*, 43.

11. Herbert McCabe comments upon the poetic image of "pitched his tent among us" as a reference to the ceremony of erecting "the tabernacle of the tent of meeting" in Exod 40:1. He considers the phrase "[dwelled] lived among us" to be "an impoverishment of St. John's words." See "Word of God," 11.

12. See chap. 2, n. 62.

13. Aimé Georges Martimort, "The Dialogue between God and His People," *The Church at Prayer: An Introduction to the Liturgy*, vol. 1, *Principles of the Liturgy* (Collegeville, MN: Liturgical Press), 152.

14. Order of Blessing of a New Lectern, no. 1175.

15. Such fruits of this *ressourcement* are so apparent in the works of scholars such as Josef Jungmann, SJ, A. G. Martimort, OP, Otto Semmelroth, SJ, Dom Gregory Dix, Yves Congar, OP, David Power, OMI, and Edward Kilmartin, SJ, to name a few of the authors that

helped to shape the Vatican II reform of the liturgy by a faithful mining of the historical sources.

16. I have written about many of these dimensions in further detail in *The Holy Preaching: The Sacramentality of the Word in the Liturgical Assembly* (Collegeville, MN: Liturgical Press, 2000) and *Standing Together in the Community of God: Liturgical Spirituality and the Presence of Christ* (Collegeville, MN: Liturgical Press, 2011). The emphasis here is on the particular role the voice plays in the sacramental Body's self-expression.

17. Lafont, *Eucharist*, 43.

18. See Otto Semmelroth in *The Preaching Word*. I have described Semmelroth's theological project in much fuller detail in *The Holy Preaching*, 20–27 and in *Standing Together in the Community of God*, 104–11. Semmelroth, a senior colleague of Karl Rahner, was a unique Catholic voice on the sacramental character of preaching in the mid-twentieth century.

19. The Eucharistic Prayers for Various Needs and Occasions clearly articulate the centrality of Christ acting as Head of this Body: "Blessed indeed is your Son, present in our midst when we are gathered by his love, and when, as once for the disciples, so now for us, he opens the Scriptures and breaks the bread."

20. See n. 5 above.

21. Lafont, *Eucharist*, 43.

22. Lectionary for Mass: Introduction, no. 7.

23. Since liturgy is poetic discourse, everything matters and forms, just as the reading of a poem "speaks volumes" beyond the mere words on the page. The text needs a voice to give it a body of meaning.

24. Otto Pächt, *Book Illumination in the Middle Ages*, trans. Kay Davenport (London: Harvey Miller Pub., 1984), 10.

25. More will be said about the place and environment in which the Body's constitutive actions take place in the following chapter.

26. Dalmais, in Martimort, *Church at Prayer*, 1:250. He credits his colleague Martimort for this insight.

27. Of the four modes of Christ's presence in the liturgy, the document notes, "Christ is always present in His Church, especially in her liturgical celebrations. He is present in the sacrifice of the Mass…in the person of His minister, 'the same now offering, through the ministry of priests, who formerly offered himself on the cross'" (citing the

Council of Trent). I have engaged this theological claim in detail in ch. 4 of *Standing Together*, 127–64.

28. For the sake of clarity, the masculine pronoun is used, but gender is not the determinant here. Rather, this charism has to do with resemblance to the heart and mind of Christ and the consequent responsibility to be the sign and representative symbol of the unity of the *totus Christus*.

29. There is a physicality to this that is part of a holistic integrity of the sacramental Body. Some have suggested that worshipers only need to conform their minds to the words and deeds of the presider to actively participate with conscious intent. This, in my opinion, is not enough and can never be enough to effect the type of sacramental Body of which I am pondering. There must be an affective bonding between presider and assembly for the Body to be whole at worship.

30. E.g., see *Catechism of the Catholic Church* 1225, noting the Congregation of Rites instruction, *Eucharisticum Mysterium*, 6.

31. See SC 51–52.

32. *Preaching the Mystery of Faith: The Sunday Homily* (Washington, DC: The United States Conference of Catholic Bishops, 2012), 30.

33. Jean Corbon uses this rich image in *The Wellspring of Worship* (Mahwah, NJ: Paulist Press, 1988). Corbon says, "If we would only determine to open the abyss within us to the abyss of God's plenitude that is offered to us: then the liturgy would no longer seem a mirage or a mere stopping place or a memory. It would become our wellspring; it would become a gushing well within us and bring us to birth as children of the Name we so greatly desire" (86). This primordial creative voice gives the Body its identity and voice.

34. Thomas Long, *The Witness of Preaching* (Louisville, KY: Westminster/John Knox Press, 2005), 177.

35. Josef Jungmann, *The Mass: An Historical, Theological, and Pastoral Survey*, trans. Julian Fernandes, SJ, ed. Mary Ellen Evans (Collegeville, MN: Liturgical Press, 1976), 180; emphasis mine. Jungmann's magisterial two-volume work, originally published in 1950, *The Mass of the Roman Rite: Its Origins and Development* [*Missarum Solemnia*], provided a key exploration into the role of worship in the tradition and attempted to clear away layers of obfuscation and historical assumptions that had accumulated over the preceding centuries. See the 1986 replica edition by Christian Classics, trans. Rev. Francis A. Brunner, CSsR (Westminster, MD, 1986).

36. Caryll Houselander, *The Reed of God* (London: Sheed and Ward, 1944; 1976), 1.

37. One could question the ritual integrity and communality of gathering the assembly in the triune name, and then uttering this invocation: "Brothers and sisters, let us acknowledge our sins, and so prepare ourselves to celebrate the sacred mysteries." The gathering itself means the new reality the liturgy proclaims has already begun. The ritual directive then adds, "A brief pause for silence follows."

38. Donghi, *Words and Gestures*, 22.

39. Donghi, *Words and Gestures*, 23.

40. I have written about this as an experience in my own Jesuit community in the epilogue to *Standing Together in the Community of God*. It is entitled "An Ecumenical Apologia: Visiting the Blessed Sacrament," 215–20.

41. St. John of the Cross, *Maxims on Love* 21, in *The Collected Works of John of the Cross*, trans. K. Kavanaugh and O. Rodriguez (Washington, DC: Institute of Carmelite Studies, 1979), 675.

42. Thomas Merton sagely remarked that "there is a higher kind of listening, which is not an attentiveness to some special wave length, a receptivity to a certain kind of message, but a general emptiness that waits to realize the fullness of the message of God within its own apparent void." This spiritual waiting of the individual contemplative, I would argue, is also a communal invitation to the Body so that she can hear and feel and taste the God for whom she longs and the Christ-life that animates her. From this perspective, the sacramental Body, to use Merton's words, waits on the word of God in silence, and when she is "answered," it is not so much by a word that bursts into silence. "It is by silence itself suddenly, inexplicably revealing itself to [her] as a word of great power, full of the voice of God." See Merton, *Contemplative Prayer* (New York: Image Books, 1971), 90.

43. St. Isaac's words are quoted in Merton's *Contemplative Prayer*, 30. There is no authorial citation, but it can be found in an earlier translation in "Good Advice Giving Instructions Concerning Watchfulness…" in Isaac of Nineveh, *Mystic Treatises* (Treatise LXV, para. 446 and 450), trans. A. J. Wensinck (Wiesbaden: Nieuwe Reeks, 1969), 299, 332.

44. Thomas Merton, *Thoughts in Solitude* [1958] (New York: Farrar, Straus, and Giroux, 1983), 91, 92.

45. Martimort, "The Dialogue between God and His People," *Church at Prayer*, 1:143. Yet, like the temptations to bifurcate silence noted above, Martimort tends to see the heart and mind and body as separate entities when he says, further on, that "the faithful may be tempted to be satisfied with aesthetic feeling and not move on to the text that the music is meant to make more attractive" (144). He cites controversies on this topic from Augustine, Basil, et al. This present work addresses that separation.

46. *Sing to the Lord: Music in Divine Worship* (Washington, DC: USCCB, 2007).

47. Maeve Louise Heaney, *Music as Theology: What Music Says about the Word*, Princeton Theological Monograph Series 184 (Eugene, OR: Pickwick Publications, 2012), 253. Using theological aesthetics, musicology, semiotics, and other contemporary communication theories, Heaney has crafted an expansive look at how all music participates in an incarnational theology, in which the paschal mystery of Christ, the ascension dynamic, and the "continued embodied presence of Christ in the Church and the world" (26) provide a model for a holistic and integrated transformational theology that embraces meaning, praxis, and mission. The conversation partners from these varied fields to which she introduces readers are itself an enriching contribution Heaney offers to theological discourse.

48. Maeve Louise Heaney, from an essay entitled "Liturgy and Lament: When Words Are Not Enough," first presented for the Jungmann Society of Jesuits and the Liturgy, St. Patrick's College Drumcondra, June 2016, Dublin, Ireland.

49. *Sing to the Lord*, 124, emphasis mine.

50. Lafont, *Eucharist*, 43. See p. 3.

51. See Rahner's "Anthropology," *Lexickon für Theologie und Kirche*, vol. 1 (Freiburg: Herder, 1957), col. 624–25.

CHAPTER 4

1. John Main, *The Christian Mysteries: Prayer and Sacrament* (Montreal: The Benedictine Priory of Montreal, 1979; rev. 1982), 32.

2. Philip Pfatteicher, *Liturgical Spirituality* (Valley Forge, PA: Trinity Press International, 1997). In his chapter entitled "Architecture:

Hallowing Space," Pfatteicher quotes the French architect Le Corbusier writing to the archbishop when his famous chapel at Ronchamp was dedicated (June 25, 1955): "Excellency: I give you this chapel of dear, faithful concrete, shaped perhaps with temerity but certainly with courage in the hope that it will seek out in you (as in those who will climb the hill) an echo of what we have drawn into it" (169).

3. Louis-Marie Chauvet, *The Sacraments: The Word of God at the Mercy of the Body* (Collegeville, MN: Liturgical Press, 2001), 105.

4. Both Mark 13:27 and Matt 24:31 use this image of the gathering of the elect from the four winds as Jesus describes the new temple that arises from the ruins of the old stones and foundations. The early Church used this imagery of the gathering in Didache 10.5: "Remember, Lord, thy Church, to deliver it from all evil and to make it perfect in thy love, and gather it together in its holiness from the four winds to thy kingdom which thou hast prepared for it. For thine is the power and the glory for ever."

5. Joining the cosmic joy echoing throughout the earth, the Exsultet gathers this praise into these walls that enfold the Body:

Rejoice, let Mother Church rejoice,
arrayed with the lightening of his glory,
let this holy building shake with joy,
filled with the mighty voices of the peoples. (*Roman Missal*, 3rd
ed., USCCB, 2011)

6. The distinction between what is sacred and what is holy may be a matter of semantics, but in the sense used here, holiness is the hallowing of the Spirit incarnate through the encounter with a lived faith of a people and the grace of God at work there.

7. Albert Rouet, *Liturgy and the Arts*, trans. Paul Philibert, OP (Collegeville, MN: Liturgical Press, 1997), 97.

8. Bert Daelemans, *Spiritus Loci: A Theological Method for Contemporary Church Architecture* (Leiden: Brill, 2015), 2, 8. The book is rich, expansive, and evocative. This chapter cannot begin to dialogue with the architectural theory and practice he uncovers, but what I have called the "synergy" of space and Body flows out of my appreciation for his work. *Synergy* is a common term in Eastern spirituality, and in work such as that of Jean Corbon, refers to "combined energies" between God and humankind that, in the power of the Holy Spirit, "conforms

160

them to Christ." The liturgy at its fullest expression of this relationship "has its source in this synergy." See Jean Corbon, *The Wellspring of Worship* (San Francisco: Ignatius Press, 2005), 7.

9. Corbon, *Wellspring*, 12.

10. Corbon, *Wellspring*, 28.

11. Considering the environment as a life-giving partner in the Body's eucharistic identity furthers de Lubac's argument that "the Eucharist and the Church are both *Corpus Christi*....The ambiguity is intentional and significant and has forceful doctrinal impact. It conveys the idea of real continuity that exists between the head and members of the unique body, and it simultaneously expresses the symbolic bond between the sacrament and the community." See Henri de Lubac, "Christian Community and Sacramental Communion," in *Theological Fragments* [*Théologies d'occasion*, 1984] (San Francisco: Ignatius Press, 1989), 72.

12. Main, *Christian Mysteries*, 31.

13. The assumption here is that the baptismal font is the threshold into the eucharistic life, and all sacramental rites—Word and Sacrament—find their trajectory in the communion celebrated at the altar of thanksgiving.

14. Mark E. Wedig and Richard S. Vosko, "The Arrangement and Furnishings of Churches for the Celebration of Eucharist," in *A Commentary on the General Instruction of the Roman Missal*, ed. Edward Foley, Nathan D. Mitchell, and Joanne M. Pierce (Collegeville, MN: Liturgical Press, 2007), 361.

15. Wedig and Vosko, "Arrangement and Furnishings of Churches," 363; emphasis mine.

16. For excellent visual examples of renovations of traditional arrangements that have been reimagined to respect the assembly's focal role, see Richard S. Vosko, *Art and Architecture for Congregational Worship: The Search for Common Ground* (Collegeville, MN: Liturgical Press, 2019), figs. 1–8.

17. Rouet, *Liturgy and the Arts*, 117.

18. Otto Semmelroth, *The Preaching Word: On the Theology of Proclamation*, trans. John Jay Hughes (New York: Herder and Herder, 1965), 252. For an extended discussion on the relationship between Word and Sacrament as the ritual embodiment of incarnation and redemption, see my *Standing Together in the Community of God: Liturgical Spirituality and the Presence of Christ* (Collegeville, MN: Liturgical Press, 2011), 108.

19. Indeed, monastic churches and parochial environments, though similar in the necessary relationship between altar and ambo, differ in physical placement when the use and the character of the assembly enters into the configuration. This does not negate the primary importance of the environment for the community's prayer but asks for an attentive intentionality to each assembly's practice and communal identity.

20. The discussion of a new hearing and a "fresh word" are discussed in Mary Catherine Hilkert's *Naming Grace: Preaching and the Sacramental Imagination* (New York: Continuum, 1997), esp. chap. 3, "Preaching as the Art of Naming Grace," 44–57. In an earlier book, I have taken this idea further by looking at the insights of New Historicist literary critics who speak of a "circulation of social energy" that makes each proclamation of a community's revered text literally "a new hearing." See my *The Holy Preaching: The Sacramentality of the Word in the Liturgical Assembly* (Collegeville, MN: Liturgical Press, 2000), see esp. 91–100. I vividly recall from my childhood the words of Psalm 95 etched into the marble of the pulpit in our parish church: "If today you hear His voice, harden not your hearts."

21. Edward Schillebeeckx, *Christ the Sacrament of the Encounter with God*, trans. Cornelius Ernst, 3rd rev. ed. (New York: Sheed, Andrews, and McMeel, 1963), 216. This groundbreaking work in sacramental theology around the time of the Vatican Council provided a foundation for the shift from static metaphysical categories describing sacraments to one of personal encounter, divine and human, and actively participating persons with each other.

22. Wedig and Vosko, "Arrangement and Furnishings of Churches," 369.

23. Louis-Marie Chauvet, *Symbol and Sacrament: A Sacramental Reinterpretation of Christian Existence*, trans. Patrick Madigan, SJ, and Madeleine Beaumont (Collegeville, MN: Liturgical Press, 1995), 190. See esp. the entire chapter 6, entitled "The Relation between Scripture and Sacrament," 190–227.

24. Otto Semmelroth, *Church and Sacrament*, trans. Emily Schlossberger (Notre Dame, IN: Fides Publishers, 1965), 38. See my *Standing Together in the Community of God*, 83. Karl Rahner used this insight to express the wholeness of Word and Sacrament as a single work bestowing grace in "The Word and the Eucharist," in *Theological Investigations*, vol. 4, trans. Kevin Smyth (New York: Crossroad,

1982), 267. The physical relationship of altar with ambo facilitates this unity of the "redemptive dialogue" in which Christ is both "Word and Answer." See n15 and Semmelroth in *The Preaching Word*, 232.

25. Chauvet, *Symbol and Sacrament*, 197.

26. Chauvet, *Symbol and Sacrament*, 219.

27. Chauvet, *Symbol and Sacrament*, 220.

28. The renovation by Robert Rambusch of St. James Cathedral in Seattle is a beautiful example of this four-cornered setting where the word is proclaimed, the cantor directs the communal song, the presider leads and collects the prayer, and the bishop's cathedra represents the unity of the diocesan Body, all are seen to come from the assembly gathered around and honoring the communion table that cements this unity with Christ and one another. Another example in a smaller setting is Holy Rosary Chapel in Adrian, MI, also redesigned in 2003 by Rambusch. See Richard S. Vosko, "The Stones Still Cry Out: The Art and Architecture of Robert E. Rambusch," *Worship* 93 (April 2019): 122–38. Bert Daelemans's *Spiritus Loci* highlights, among others, St. François de Molitor in Paris, France, designed by Corinne Callies and Jean-Marie Duthilleul in 2005, and St. Gregory of Nyssa Episcopal Church in San Francisco, designed by John Goldman in 1995. See Daelemans, "Eucharistic Space: Dance and Garden," in *Spritus Loci*, 251–313.

29. Vosko, *Art and Architecture for Congregational Worship*, 47.

30. Cyril of Jerusalem, Cat. 21, *Mystagogica* 3, 1–3: PG 33, 1087–91.

31. Rouet, *Liturgy and the Arts*, 168.

32. Chauvet's four traits of a symbol, noted earlier, "(1) fitting together, (2) crystallization, (3) recognition (or identification), and (4) submission to the communal Other," are especially helpful in observing how a living symbol speaks and responds in a liturgical space. See *Sacraments*, 70ff.

33. Maxwell Johnson cites the following as focal for truly claiming our baptismal identity in his article entitled "Back Home to the Font: Eight Implications for a Baptismal Spirituality," *Worship* 71, no. 6 (November 1997): 482–504. They are, briefly,

A re-claiming of baptism as the radical equalizer

A re-evaluation of the relationship between baptism and "Confirmation"

An advocacy for and the practice of the communion of all the baptized

A renewed stance against creeping Pelagianism

A renewed sense of the baptismal focus at the center of the liturgical year

A renewed sense of both lay and ordained ministry

A renewed sense and zeal for ecumenism

A renewed sense of all Christian life as a living out of baptism

34. Herbert Vorgrimler notes that the three sacraments that bestow a "sacramental character" (baptism, confirmation, and orders) emphasize the intrinsic relationship between the sacraments and the ecclesial reality they express. This "character," as both the Council of Florence and Trent acknowledged, "indicates that 'spiritual and indelible sign'…that is marked on the soul." The importance of this, especially for a consideration of baptismal identity, is that it is forever "a witness to the fact of the initiative of God, which lays hold of human beings, (and) anticipates every human decision." Key to this pure gift and character is "likeness to Christ" and membership in ecclesial life. See Herbert Vorgrimler, *Sacramental Theology*, trans. Linda M. Maloney (Collegeville, MN: Liturgical Press, 1992), 92–93.

35. Vosko, *Art and Architecture for Congregational Worship*, 117.

36. Vosko, *Art and Architecture for Congregational Worship*, 119. Vosko's book is a helpful example of many architects' arguments that different styles and intentions about a sacred space can still engage the present time in which they are inhabited, bringing the disparate parts of a community together, simply by "renovating" what excludes, detracts, and diminishes the unity of the common, holy people of God.

37. Eucharistic Prayers for Use in Masses for Various Needs I–IV, *Roman Missal* 3rd ed.

38. See n. 32 above and Chauvet, *Sacraments*, 70.

39. See esp. chap. 4 in *Standing Together*, 133. The entire chapter explores this theme of "gatherer."

40. Male personal pronouns are used here. As I have written elsewhere, this apostolic charism should not be based on gender, but on fidelity to Christ's word and the Spirit who gives life (see Luke 11:28 and John 6:63). We pray for the day…suffice it to say that.

41. For a rich discussion on the "Gratuitousness and Graciousness" of the triune God and the liturgy as a "fundamental aim" of this freely given divine grace that impels the assembly "into the mystery of Christ's Passover," see Chauvet, *Sacraments*, 86–89.

42. Janowiak, *Standing Together*, 127. The perichoretic dance of the Trinity, where each person always acts in consort with the others, is a pattern that highlights the graceful movement of the Body at prayer. And the beauty and harmony of musical expression provides an imaginary voice for this liturgical synergy.

43. Both theologians have articulated the ecclesial identity of the priest/presider in ways that correspond to the role of the "gatherer" expressed here. See David Power, "Representing Christ in Community and Sacrament," in *Being a Priest Today*, ed. Donald J. Goergen, OP (Collegeville, MN: Liturgical Press, 1992); and Susan K. Wood, *Sacramental Orders*, ed. John D. Laurance, *Lex Orandi* Series (Collegeville, MN: Liturgical Press, 2000). Other important sacramental theologians that helped to reorient the view of sacramental priesthood from its ontological foundations to a mutuality of symbolic roles can be found in *Standing Together*, chap. 4. Of particular note are Louis Marie Chauvet's *Symbol and Sacrament* and Kenan Osborne's *Priesthood: A History of the Ordained Ministry in the Roman Catholic Church*. The dismantling of the ontological metaphysical approach to sacraments is a much larger discussion, of course. For an example of recent scholarship, see Andrew Prevot, *Thinking Prayer: Theology and Spirituality amid the Crisis of Modernity* (Notre Dame, IN: University of Notre Dame Press, 2015).

44. Rouet, *Liturgy and the Arts*, 95.

45. Rouet, *Liturgy and the Arts*, 95–96.

46. Vosko, *Art and Architecture*, 149.

47. Vosko, *Art and Architecture*, 150.

48. Vosko, *Art and Architecture*, 151, 150.

49. Joyce Ann Zimmerman, *The Ministry of the Assembly* (Collegeville, MN: Liturgical Press, 2016), 40.

50. See n. 28 above.

51. Order of Dedication of a Church and an Altar (ODCA), 364.

52. See John 4. Corbon calls this symbolic well of the liturgy as the place where "two thirsts meet" (24).

53. Corbon, *Wellspring of Worship*, 37.

54. Daelemans, *Spiritus Loci*, 254–55.

55. New Historian literary critic Stephen Greenblatt speaks of "cultural artifacts" that are alive by engaging in any time and place the life of those who engage them. In his words, such artifacts "do not stay still…they are bound up with personal and institutional conflicts,

negotiations, and appropriations." See Greenblatt, "Resonance and Wonder," in *Shakespearean Negotiations: Essays in Early Modern Culture* (New York: Routledge, 1990), 161–83. I have used this in *Standing Together in the Community of God* to speak of the resonance of sacred texts proclaimed in the liturgical assembly (111–12), but such vibrancy and relational negotiation, I believe, happens in the liturgical environment as well, the *eucharistic* space of which Daelemans speaks.

56. Didache 10.2, 8–10.

57. Rouet, *Liturgy and the Arts*, 108.

58. Matt 17:1–9 and Mark 9:1–9.

59. See esp. Jean Corbon, *Wellspring of Worship*, 59ff. In this passage, Corbon makes the point that is at the heart of this present work: "Because human beings are their bodies, they are also, like their God, related to other persons, the cosmos, time, and him who is communion in its fullest possible form" (59–60). Further, the Eastern Christian tradition on the transfiguration and the liturgy is expressed eloquently in Corbon's meditative reflection upon the transfiguration as "the historical and literary center of the gospel by reason of its mysterious realism." Alexander Schmemann speaks of the Sunday feast as "a movement from Mount Tabor into the world, from the world into the 'day without evening' of the world to come." See Alexander Schmemann, *For the Life of the World* (Crestwood, NY: St. Vladimir's Seminary Press, 1988), 52.

60. Main, *Christian Mysteries*, 32.

61. Vosko, *Art and Architecture*, 172.

EPILOGUE

1. Jean Corbon, in *The Wellspring of Worship* (Mahwah, NJ: Paulist Press, 1988), 143.

2. Corbon, *Wellspring of Worship*, 25.

3. Louis Bouyer, *The Meaning of the Monastic Life* (London: Burns and Oates, 1955), 29. Cited in David Fagerberg, *On Liturgical Asceticism* (Washington, DC: CUA Press, 2013), 7. Bouyer (1913–2004) was influential in Vatican II scholarship and also struggled with the aftermath of the reform, much as his colleague Henri de Lubac, SJ. The dynamism he uses here is of lifeblood drawn in, renewed, and poured out, a fitting image for this liturgy of the heart in the sacramen-

tal Body. Fagerberg draws the "spatial metaphor" from his own reading of, among others, Dante's *The Divine Comedy 3: Paradise* and Dionysius the Areopagite's *The Celestial Hierarchy*, 3.2; see Fagerberg, *Liturgical Asceticism*, 5–8.

4. Fagerberg reminds us that this "dance of love and mutual indwelling of the Trinity" is our participation in the love that is the heart force of the Trinity itself. See Fagerberg, *Liturgical Asceticism*, 8.

5. John of the Cross, in *Letter* 8 to the Carmelite sisters of Beas (November 22, 1587), suggests the balance contemporary apostolic communities need for a unified centeredness by honoring silence as a place where God speaks in a special way. He tells the sisters, "Our greatest need is to be silent before this great God, silent in spirit and silent with the tongue; for his only language, the one he hears, is the silent language of love." Cited and translated in Iain Matthew, OCD, *John of the Cross: Seasons of Prayer* (Oxford: Teresian Press, 2014), 33.

6. This appellation of prayer comes from Matthew, *John of the Cross*, 32.

7. John of the Cross, *The Spiritual Canticle—Redaction A 37:3*, in Matthew, *John of the Cross*, 32.

INDEX

Index